WALKING TOURS
OF WISCONSIN'S HISTORIC TOWNS

D1312290

by Lucy Rhodes, Elizabeth McBride and Anita Matcha

Wisconsin Trails
Madison, Wisconsin

First edition, first printing
© 1998 Wisconsin Tales & Trails, Inc.

Library of Congress Catalog Card Number: 98-75060
ISBN: 0-915024-67-5

Printed in Canada by Friesens
Editor: Chris Roerden
Designer: Kathie Campbell
Cover Illustration and Maps: Pamela Harden
Research: Carole Zellie

Special Thanks
This project has been funded in part by the Wisconsin Sesquicentennial Commission,
with funds from the State of Wisconsin, and individual and corporate contributors.
We'd like to express our appreciation for the generosity of these corporations
and recognize their contributions. For a complete list of contributors see page 112.

Wisconsin Tales & Trails, Inc.
P.O. Box 5650
Madison, WI   53705
(800) 236-8088
info@wistrails.com

To the thousands of Wisconsinites who,
by their dedicated efforts to preserve our historic buildings,
help bring the past alive.

Bayfield

Hudson
Chippewa Falls
Eau Claire

Wausau

Ephraim

Sturgeon Bay

Stockholm
Alma

Stevens Point

Green Bay

Rural

Appleton

La Crosse

Berlin

Plymouth
Sheboygan Falls

Portage
Baraboo

Cedarburg

Watertown

Madison

Milwaukee

Mineral Point
Cassville

Cooksville
Evansville
Platteville   Janesville

Racine
Whitewater

Lake Geneva   Kenosha

Contents

Introduction

⌃

There is no better way to explore a town than on foot, and no better town to explore than one that is rich in history and architecture. Wisconsin's landscape is filled with such towns. Those included in this book share two attributes: historic significance and a substantial number of attractive buildings with original architecture intact or restored. We hope that by visiting these communities readers will deepen their knowledge of Wisconsin history, and perhaps be inspired with a new dedication toward preserving historic buildings. For it is these very buildings that tell the story of Wisconsin's settlement, from the miners' cottages in Mineral Point to the lumber barons' lavish mansions in Eau Claire—enduring testimony to years of courage and enterprise since statehood in 1848.

Brief descriptions of each community are presented here, accompanied by a map. The walking routes are fairly short—pleasant strolls through residential neighborhoods and commercial districts—but readers always have the option of venturing beyond the next corner. And for more detailed information, there is a list of organizations to contact in the back of the book.

Alma

*An engaging river town, with
a dramatic view of the mighty Mississippi*

Mark Twain would have felt at home in Alma. A diminutive town spread along the banks of the Mississippi River, it seems perpetually charmed by the mighty waterway that flows so intimately beside it. Main Street is a collage of 19th-century brick mercantile buildings. Turn-of-the-century houses sit on terraces wedged between the Mississippi and looming Twelve Mile Bluff. Lock and Dam No. 4, in the middle of "downtown," heaves big barges upriver. During fall and spring migration, flocks of tundra swans soar overhead, seeking a resting place in the nearby sloughs, just as they have for centuries.

Early white settlers came to the area—at the time, a near-roadless wilderness—by steamboat in 1848. These Swiss immigrants made their living cutting wood for steamboat fuel. Settlers inland grew wheat, and for a while Alma thrived as a ship-

**Neumeister Building facade,
305 S. Main St.**

ping port for grain. When lumbering boomed a few decades later, log rafting became Alma's major industry. In the 1880s, Beef Slough, north of Alma, was the largest log harbor in the world, a collecting point for the huge rafts of timber that spilled downstream from the lumber camps.

Today, Alma is a wonderful place to stroll, compact, with stairways taking you up and down its short streets. Almost the entire village is listed on the National Register of Historic Places. Alma is not, however, frilly and quaint. While some historic buildings have been restored, others are worn and sagging; many have modern false fronts that obscure their age and design. Alma stands as it always has: without pretension—a river town proudly weathered by time and circumstance.

Main Street, about six blocks long, parallels the Mississippi. The commercial district is anchored

1

by the Tester & Polin Mercantile Store (1861) at 215 N. Main Street, one of several local grain exchanges at which farmers traded their harvest for vouchers that could be used to buy supplies. Notice the building's arched windows, brick exterior

Carl Urfer House, 609 S. Second St.

and overhanging balcony, architectural details that are repeated often throughout Alma. The Burlington Hotel (1891) at 809 N. Main Street is also a landmark; brick-veneered with a zinc cornice, it was patronized by railroad employees as well as the traveling public. Farmers bringing their grain to Alma stayed overnight at the Sherman House (1866) at 301 S. Main Street, a hotel that also boasted a lively saloon.

Residences, many built in the ornate Queen Anne style, line Second Street, one block up the bluff. The family home of Anton Walser, the architect who, with his brother, Ulrich, designed most of Alma's significant buildings, is the large three-story Victorian (1897) at 600 S. Second Street. The massive Buffalo County Training School at 505 S. Second Street was built by Walser in 1902. The school trained teachers until 1967; it is now the City Hall. The Walser brothers also designed the impressive Peter and Mathilda Ibach Residence (1897) at 108 S. Second Street. Ibach, a successful store owner who organized Alma's German American Bank, demanded that his home be constructed of the finest lumber. A cornerstone-laying ceremony featured music by the Alma Brass Band and the Frohsinn Singing Society.

From Second Street, a wooded path winds up Twelve Mile Bluff to Buena Vista Park and one of the finest views in Wisconsin. From this high perch, Alma, directly below, seems a small hub of civilization. The bluffs of Minnesota are a tangle of rocks and trees, and the slate-blue Mississippi flows broad and full below. You'll likely see eagles and turkey vultures soaring by at eye level on the river valley's strong air currents.

Begin your walk at the Tester and Polin Mercantile Store near the intersection of Main and Cedar streets. Head south on Main Street to view 19th-century commercial buildings. Turn left on North Street and climb the bluffside stairs to Second Street. Explore this residential district by turning right on Second and walking as far as Oak Street. Then reverse direction and follow Second Street in the opposite direction, heading north. Turn right on Elm Street to reach the Buena Vista Trail. The walk up the bluff requires some effort but is not as steep as you might suspect. After enjoying the view, retrace your steps down the trail, then proceed straight on Elm Street, which takes you back to Main Street, close to where you began this walk.

Appleton

Queen of the Fox River Valley

One of the few rivers in North America to flow north, the Fox River rushes from Lake Winnebago to Green Bay through a valley of bedrock created by the glaciers. Recognizing the hydraulic power to be harnessed from the lower Fox, European settlers built a series of locks and dams in the 1850s, which provided power to mills to saw up the bounty of the North Woods. By the time the northern pines were logged out, the Fox River Valley turned to paper manufacturing. Within a 15-mile stretch of the valley, corporations such as Kimberly-Clark, Menasha Corporation, James River and Fox River all produce every type of paper imaginable—thus the region's title, Paper Valley.

Appleton is the central city of this paper empire. Though its heart is industrial, Appleton's residential neighborhoods are wooded and quiet, spilling down to the river from College Avenue, down-

**Italianate Duplex,
414-416 S. State St.**

town's main artery. Lovely homes line streets that once were Indian footpaths, reflecting architectural styles that span the eras from Victorian to Bauhaus.

The wealthy industrialists built their residences along Prospect Avenue, overlooking the river and their mills and factories below. Merchants and town officials located themselves closer to downtown, in the blocks between Prospect and College avenues. Today, this district is referred to as the Third Ward, containing the homes of Appleton's Yankee, Irish and German settlers.

The grande dame of the mansions lining Prospect Avenue is a massive Queen Anne called Hearthstone (1881-82) at 625 W. Prospect. Designed as an architectural showplace, the home became the world's first to be powered by a central hydroelectric plant in September 1882. The original electroliers and light switches designed by Thomas Edison are still in use today, and the

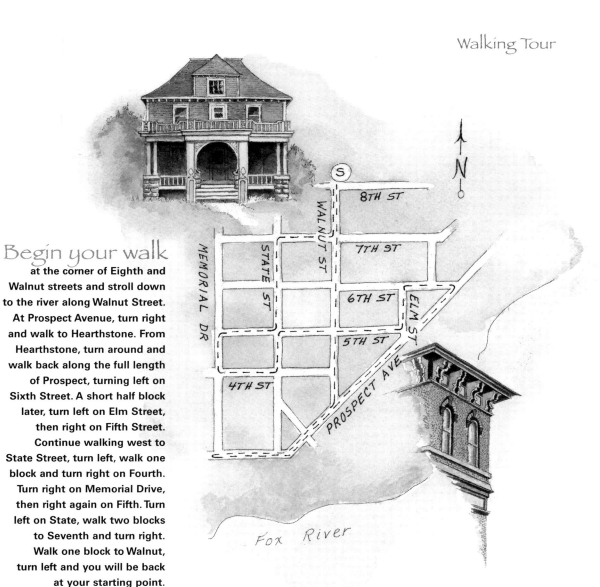

Begin your walk

at the corner of Eighth and Walnut streets and stroll down to the river along Walnut Street. At Prospect Avenue, turn right and walk to Hearthstone. From Hearthstone, turn around and walk back along the full length of Prospect, turning left on Sixth Street. A short half block later, turn left on Elm Street, then right on Fifth Street. Continue walking west to State Street, turn left, walk one block and turn right on Fourth. Turn right on Memorial Drive, then right again on Fifth. Turn left on State, walk two blocks to Seventh and turn right. Walk one block to Walnut, turn left and you will be back at your starting point.

home's lavish Victorian furnishings have been preserved—including the nine tiled fireplaces for which the home was named. The home is open to the public throughout the year for tours.

Grout block Italianate, 523 S. State St.

Hearthstone's neighbors on Prospect Avenue exhibit a variety of tastes and styles. The villa at 315 W. Prospect (1870), trimmed in ornate details, looks as though it would be more at home in the Italian countryside than on the banks of a Wisconsin river. The home is testimony to the prominence of its owner, John Whorton, vice president and manager of the Fox River Paper Company. One of Appleton's founding fathers, Theodore Conkey, built the Italianate home (1849) at 433 W. Prospect. Conkey served terms in the Wisconsin State Senate and General Assembly in the early years of statehood. What you see today is only the central portion of the original home. The summer kitchen that existed on the east side of the home was demolished in 1914, and a west wing was moved.

Walking away from the river, be sure not to miss the tiny Greek Revival cottage (circa 1851) at 515 W. Fifth. Almost lost among its more modern neighbors, this is a rare example of a pioneer vernacular cottage. A foursquare Italianate (1868) colored in soft pink occupies the corner lot at Fifth and State. The home was built in 1868 using an experimental mixture of lime and gravel, and survives today as a rare example of this "grout block." A 1907 Colonial Revival at 617 S. State stands out because of its circular porch entrance; the brick Tudor Revival (1891) at 707 S. State is impressive in its massive size.

What may have been Appleton's first duplex (1881) is located at 414-416 S. State. Tidy brick buildings in the Italianate style, the twin homes were joined together along a common back wall when constructed. The homes were separated in 1913 to generate better rents, but they remain mirror images of each other.

Baraboo

A pastoral town
with a colorful circus heritage

Nestled amidst the hills of Sauk County, Baraboo is one of the few Wisconsin towns laid out around a central square, following New England tradition. Here, Courthouse Square, a shady park complete with benches, is framed by commercial buildings whose storefronts show off late—19th-century architectural details. The city's early economic success came from mills established along the Baraboo River—at one time 17 mills were operating on the river—and from thriving retail enterprises downtown.

The building on the southeast corner of Oak and Fourth streets housed the oldest family business in town. A German immigrant, August Reinking, bought and remodeled this building in 1879 and opened a dry goods business. Members of the Reinking family operated businesses from this site for more than a century. Baraboo's oldest retail business, a drugstore, opened in 1858 on the southeast corner of Oak and Third streets. The present corner structure dates from 1880, after fire destroyed the original building. The Taylor Book Store was established in 1896 at 512 Oak Street; the building retains the original period woodwork and hardwood floors. Area history is further evident in the sandstone friezes on the outside wall of the courthouse annex. Carved panels highlight episodes of Baraboo's history from 18th-century exploration through its circus heyday.

It was Baraboo's famous native sons, the Ringling Brothers, who left an indelible mark on this little town. Sons of a local harness maker, the brothers organized the Ringling Brothers Classic and Comic Concert Company in 1882, and held the first performance in nearby Mazomanie. Steadily successful, the show was renamed "Ringling Bros. World's

Detail in Courthouse wall coping.

Greatest Shows" in 1884, and moved about from town to town in wagons rented from area farmers. Eventually the Ringlings bought out Bailey, securing title to "The Greatest Show on Earth." The circus wintered in Baraboo in buildings along Water Street, many of which still stand and are located

Northeast corner of Broadway and 4th Ave., original home of the *Baraboo Republic* newspaper.

on the grounds of the Circus World Museum.

The circus moved to Connecticut in 1918, but left a lasting legacy in Baraboo, the most outstanding of which is the Al Ringling Theater, located at 136 Fourth Avenue. Al and his wife, Lou, spent $100,000 in the early 1900s to build a theater and auditorium similar to European palaces. The auditorium is a one-third scale model of the great opera hall of Versailles; the entrance lobby contains a replica of the Choir Boys' Frieze designed in 1671 for the Cathedral at Florence. The theater opened in 1915 and hosted performances of international renown until 1927. The theater was partially restored in 1978-80, and its opulence is still evident in the gold leaf and painted murals throughout the interior. Al and Lou's home (1905) was located a block from downtown on the corner of Fifth and Broadway. Built of red stone, the Renaissance-style mansion features towering chimneys, art-glass windows and a pillared porte-cochere.

Baraboo slumbers peacefully now, but walking the streets of downtown one can't help but imagine the excitement generated by the Greatest Show on Earth during the days when it filled the little town with elephants, zebras and clowns.

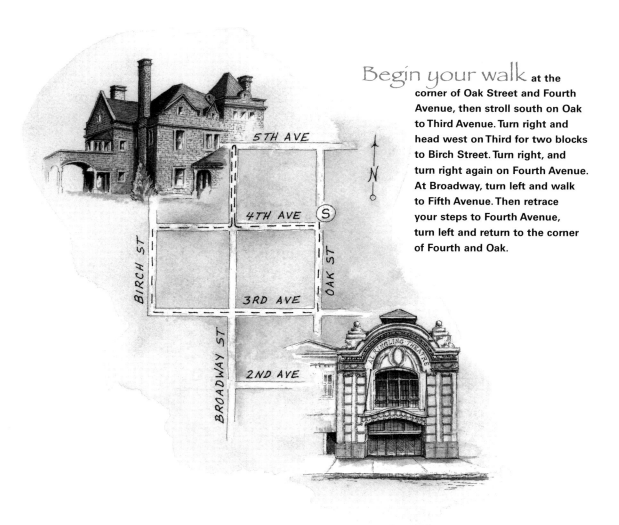

Begin your walk at the corner of Oak Street and Fourth Avenue, then stroll south on Oak to Third Avenue. Turn right and head west on Third for two blocks to Birch Street. Turn right, and turn right again on Fourth Avenue. At Broadway, turn left and walk to Fifth Avenue. Then retrace your steps to Fourth Avenue, turn left and return to the corner of Fourth and Oak.

5TH AVE

4TH AVE

3RD AVE

2ND AVE

BIRCH ST

OAK ST

BROADWAY ST

N

S

AL RINGLING THEATRE

Bayfield

A pristine fishing village overlooking the Apostle Islands

erched on a hillside that drops straight down to Lake Superior, Bayfield is one of the most attractive villages in the state. The small downtown faces a busy, deep-water harbor filled with fishing and pleasure craft. Victorian houses with open wraparound porches sit high above town, commanding spectacular lake views dominated by the Apostle Islands.

The area's first settlers were the Ojibwe, who arrived on Madeline Island in the late 15th century. They lived on the island until the early 1600s when, legend states, the spirits of human sacrifices drove them to the mainland. The French arrived soon after, establishing a fur trade on the island that flourished until the 1800s. By that time, the area was discovered by entrepre-

**Allen C. Fuller House,
301 Rittenhouse Ave.**

neurs with big dreams.

Lt. Henry Bayfield of the British Navy made the first charts of Lake Superior and the islands between 1823 and 1825. Henry Rice, a friend of Bayfield's and a member of the Minnesota Legislature, took Bayfield's charts to Washington, D.C., where he convinced investors of the potential of the deep-water harbor between Madeline Island and the mainland. Rice believed this site would be the greatest port on Lake Superior, eclipsing Duluth and Chicago. The investors formed the Bayfield Land Company and platted a town in the wilderness in 1856. Within weeks the first schooner arrived with the town's first settlers.

Though it never became the port of Rice's dreams, Bayfield did grow into an active shipping port. By the late 1800s the lumber industry was producing millions of board feet annually, fisheries were booming, and brownstone quarries were supplying stone for rowhouses in Chicago and New York City. When the railroad arrived in 1883, it brought tourism with it, as did the excursion boats from Buffalo, Detroit and Chicago. Wealthy residents and vacationers built grand homes on the hillside looking out over the water.

But Bayfield's prosperity was short-lived, putting an end to the dreams of the town's founders. The railroad established Washburn as its principal Lake Superior port in 1883, and Washburn was designated the county seat in 1892. The lumber and brownstone industries disappeared, and though commercial fishing remained, it never again reached the same economic heights as it had in the late 19th century. Today, only fishing, limited agriculture and tourism have remained to provide an economic base for this Lake Superior village.

But therein lies its charm. Precisely because "progress" passed it by, most of Bayfield today remains as it was in its heyday.

The majority of buildings in Bayfield were built of wood. The lumber industry provided seemingly unlimited material for the hillside clapboard homes and for the false fronts in the business district. Downtown focuses on the waterfront while the residential district climbs up the sandstone

William Knight House, 108 N. Third St.

bluff at the town's back. The wealthy of Bayfield spared no lavishness when they built their grand Queen Annes-elaborate ornamentation and irregular profiles, stained glass and decorative siding, all were put to use, and all, of course, looked lakeward for the spectacular view. The Boutin house (1908), 7 Rice Avenue, and the Fuller House (1890), 301 Rittenhouse Avenue, are splendid examples of Bayfield's finest. Both homes feature extensive wraparound porches, gabled roofs, bay and dormer windows, towers, turrets and decorative work in a variety of materials. The Boutin house remains an immaculate private residence while the Fuller house has been turned into an elegant bed-and-breakfast, the Old Rittenhouse Inn.

Interspersed among the grande dames are the clapboard homes of the Scandinavian and German immigrants who came to Bayfield to work in the lumber industry. Though smaller and simpler in design, these homes also feature open porches and reflect a coastal charm. Most are graced with decorative gingerbread trim-attributed to the immigrant carpenters. A wonderful example of a whimsical choice of trim is found on Christ Episcopal Church (1870), 125 N. Third Street. The eaves of this little building are dripping with scrollwork, giving it a country cottage air. The first Episcopal Church built in northern Wisconsin, this is one of Bayfield's oldest structures.

Though Bayfield's quarries provided stone for thousands of rowhouses in Chicago and New York City, there are only a handful of brownstone buildings in Bayfield—most notably the former county courthouse on Washington Avenue, and the Holy Family Catholic Church at the top of Second Street.

D.J. Etsell Building, 225 Rittenhouse Ave.

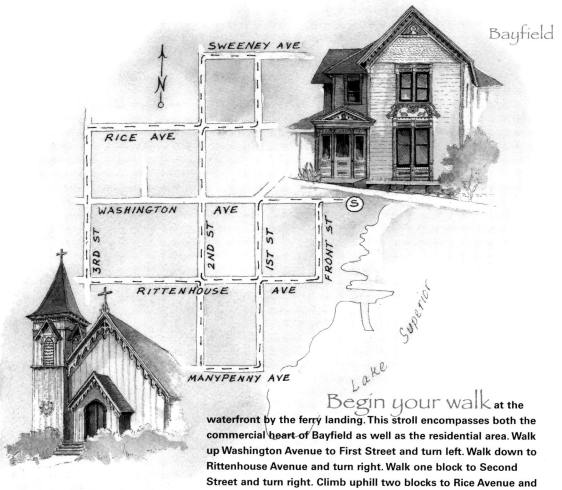

Begin your walk at the waterfront by the ferry landing. This stroll encompasses both the commercial heart of Bayfield as well as the residential area. Walk up Washington Avenue to First Street and turn left. Walk down to Rittenhouse Avenue and turn right. Walk one block to Second Street and turn right. Climb uphill two blocks to Rice Avenue and turn right. Turn left on First Street and walk to the top of the hill. Turn left on Sweeney Avenue, then left again on Second Street and walk downhill to Rice Avenue. Turn right on Rice Avenue and walk over the Old Iron Bridge (this is not for those who suffer vertigo!), then turn left on Third Street and continue walking downhill to Rittenhouse Avenue. Turn left, walk two blocks and turn right on Second. Turn left on Manypenny Avenue, walk one block, turn left on First Street and walk one block. Turn right on Rittenhouse, left on Front and you will be back at the parking lot.

Berlin

Home to magnificent Victorians

Turning off the highway into the residential area of Berlin, you come upon Nathan Strong Park, a city block of cut grass and trees. Pleasant, but nothing out of the ordinary for a small Wisconsin town. Then you notice the homes surrounding the park on all four sides—imposing 19th-century homes one after another, immaculate in condition, varied in style. All at once Berlin becomes atypical.

Tucked into the northeast corner of Green Lake County, Berlin was founded in 1847 with a town site laid out on top of a glacier-shaved stump of a prehistoric granite mountain. The

Gothic Revival, 169 E. Park Ave.

granite was quarried as early as 1884, producing stone called Berlin ryolite, the hardest stone in the world. Though the stone was used mainly for street paving, several buildings throughout the town feature the stone in their construction.

Berlin never achieved the stature of the paper mill Fox River towns, but small businesses and enterprises have provided a solid economic base since the town was founded. Serving as testimony are the homes in the Nathan Strong Park neighborhood, built primarily by local merchants.

The most noticeable home facing the park is the bright blue and white Queen Anne (1882) located at 209 E. Park. The town's brochure calls the home "exuberant"—an apt description, as this home features a number of porches, bays and decorative touches. Though the neighboring homes are a bit more subdued they are no less remarkable, exhibiting a gamut of architectural styles.

On the corner of Huron and State streets are twin Italianate homes (1872)—unique in that they are mirror images of each other. Brothers Horace

Begin your walk on E. Park Avenue at
the northwest corner of Nathan Strong Park. Walk around the
block clockwise, turning right on Church Street, right on E.
Huron, and right on State Street. Walk to E. Park and turn left.
Walk down Park to N. Adams Street and turn right. Walk to E.
Moore Street and turn right, then turn right on Oak Street. Turn
left on E. Noyes, then right on State Street. You will be back to
your starting point when you reach Park Avenue.

and Henry Miner, married to sisters, built the brick homes next to each other. An impressive Romanesque Revival (1893) resides at the corner of Park Avenue and State Street, built of brick and flaunting a huge turret on the front. One of Berlin's old-

the park boundaries, many of which line N. Adams Street. Berlin's first attorney built the lovely brick home at 156 N. Adams Street in 1858. Italianate in style, notice the cornice brackets, matching trim on the cupola and the original-style porch across

Brick Italianate, 156 N. Adams St.

Romanesque Revival, 181 E. Park Ave.

est residences (1849) sits farther along Park Avenue at 169 E. Park. Though smaller and less pretentious than its neighbors, don't pass it by. A Gothic Revival, the home sports original barge board trim, gingerbread trim along the eaves, and arch-styled windows and front door.

There are more homes to be discovered beyond

the front. Across the street is Berlin's lone example of neoclassical. The sweeping façade accented by columns gives this home an illusion of grandeur, overshadowing the plain 1859 Italianate next door. Built of brick, with some inside partitions as thick as 18 inches, this home once featured elaborate trim, later removed.

Cassville

A tenacious little river town that once thought
it should be the state capital

Created in 1831 with the construction of a lone general store, Cassville for many years was overshadowed by its neighbor, Potosi—a lead-mining boomtown and the largest port on the upper Mississippi at the time. (By 1850 real estate in Potosi was the most valuable in the state.) However, Potosi's fortunes eventually changed when the Grant River silted in, making it unnavigable, and lead mining declined. As if waiting in the wings like an understudy, Cassville took over the lucrative river traffic trade and prospered—until the railroad and barge traffic passed it by in favor of larger cities.

Cassville is a little shabby around the edges today, but visitors discover some historic gems among modern homes and behind peeling paint. Crunched between sandstone bluffs and the Mississippi, the town runs long and narrow, only three blocks wide. Most know Cassville for its ferry,

Greek Revival, 313 Frederick St.

which operates daily from May to October carrying cars and people across the river to Iowa. One of the few car ferries remaining in the U.S., the first plowed across the river in 1836—the same year a location was sought for the capital of the Wisconsin Territory. Cassville locals championed their village, attracting land speculators who hoped to make a killing in real estate. The Daniels-Denniston Company from New York built the Denniston House (1836) on Front Street to accommodate politicians.

When Madison was chosen over Cassville, the building went into decline until purchased by a former state governor, Nelson Dewey, in 1855. Dewey converted the brick building into a hotel, and it operated until 1985 when it was converted into apartments. Many features of the building have been removed over the years, but the Denniston house still commands a clear view of the Mississippi, and if you look closely you can still see the original bricklaying pattern on the side wall.

A block up from Front Street, Amelia Street cuts a swath through the three-block business district. Many of the storefronts have been modernized, but cornice and window treatments and

Sherman Boarding House, 117 W. Front St.

brick facades remain true to the late 1800s. Many homes and businesses in Cassville were constructed of "Barrows Brick," which came from a local brickyard owned by Joe Barrow. Barrow's home (circa 1870), made of brick, of course, is located at the end of the retail district at 217 Wiota Street, and it remains substantially original.

The highlights of Cassville's past are found along tree-shaded Dewey Street, one block over from Amelia. The imposing brick home at 401 Frederick (1888) has walls 16-inches thick. A wrought iron fence encloses the yard, lending an air of elegance and privacy to the mansion. Farther down Dewey, behind a white picket fence, the lovely Greek Revival (1855) at 401 Denniston looks almost untouched since its construction. The exterior is mostly original and retains its detailing; note the six-over-six windows. The former Town Hall (1889) is located just up the street at the corner of Bluff and Denniston. The multi-windowed building wears its age well, despite the modern apartment touches.

Cassville's churches are also worthy of note. The United Methodist Church between Wall and Frederick streets on Dewey is an excellent example of early ecclesiastical construction with an original exterior. The red brick River Valley Community Church at 402 Denniston was dedicated in 1880, and has changed little since then. The bell in the steeple was installed in 1885, purchased for $128.

Cassville is a town where youngsters ride bikes down the middle of the street, unafraid of traffic—for there is none. It slumbers quietly, and as the sun slants across homefronts turning the bricks terra cotta, it's easy to see why the town's founders thought the spot worthy to be the state capital.

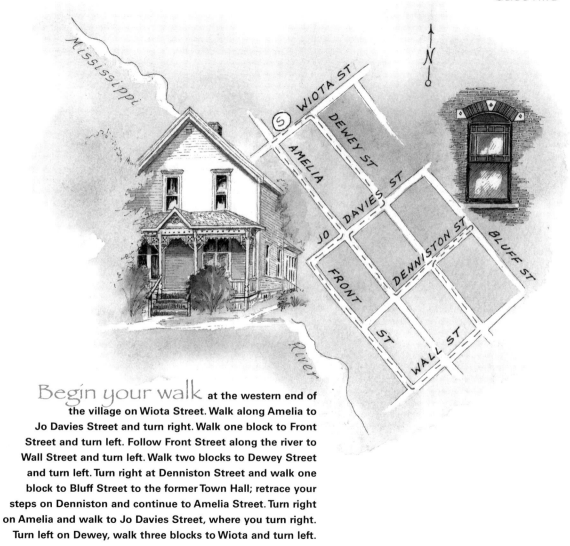

Begin your walk at the western end of
the village on Wiota Street. Walk along Amelia to
Jo Davies Street and turn right. Walk one block to Front
Street and turn left. Follow Front Street along the river to
Wall Street and turn left. Walk two blocks to Dewey Street
and turn left. Turn right at Denniston Street and walk one
block to Bluff Street to the former Town Hall; retrace your
steps on Denniston and continue to Amelia Street. Turn right
on Amelia and walk to Jo Davies Street, where you turn right.
Turn left on Dewey, walk three blocks to Wiota and turn left.

Cedarburg

A handsome mill town, lovingly restored

Cedarburg has been blessed with what the fashion industry calls "good bones." Its commercial district was built primarily of stone: golden limestone and yellow-tinged Cream City brick. Thus, its "skeleton" is sturdy and straight. And in the soft light of a summer evening, Cedarburg's main street positively glows.

Like many Wisconsin communities, the town began with a mill. Friederich Hilgen and Walter Schroeder cleared a road into the frontier north of Milwaukee, built a small grist mill along the rushing Cedar Creek, then wrote to their German relatives, luring them to the new land. Settlers came. In 1855 the two founders replaced their mill with one that was five stories high. Ten years later they erected yet another— the Cedarburg Woolen Mill—at the north end of town. Employing 60 workers, it was the only pro-

Diedrich Wittenberg House, W64 N707 Washington Ave.

ducer of worsted yarns west of Philadelphia. By the late 19th century, Cedarburg's population was almost entirely German. Superior masons, they filled the town with stone buildings of local limestone and the cream-colored brick particular to the Milwaukee region.

The 20th century, however, brought great change. Workers discovered that Cedarburg lay within easy commuting distance of Milwaukee, and between 1940 and 1960 the population more than doubled. Developers, under the banner of modernization, began tearing down the distinctive but old-fashioned buildings. A wind-powered grist mill—the only such mill in Wisconsin—was razed. So was Turner Hall, once the center of German social life.

When the wrecking ball threatened St. Francis Borgia Church and the Cedarburg Woolen Mill it-

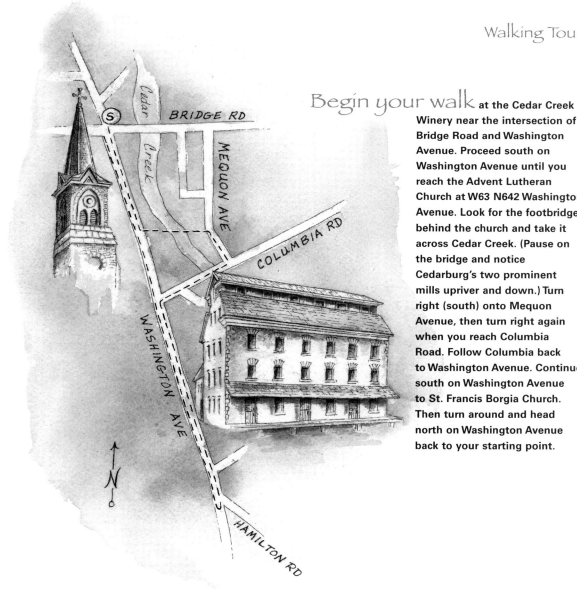

Begin your walk at the Cedar Creek Winery near the intersection of Bridge Road and Washington Avenue. Proceed south on Washington Avenue until you reach the Advent Lutheran Church at W63 N642 Washington Avenue. Look for the footbridge behind the church and take it across Cedar Creek. (Pause on the bridge and notice Cedarburg's two prominent mills upriver and down.) Turn right (south) onto Mequon Avenue, then turn right again when you reach Columbia Road. Follow Columbia back to Washington Avenue. Continue south on Washington Avenue to St. Francis Borgia Church. Then turn around and head north on Washington Avenue back to your starting point.

self, citizens decided to buck the trend. Over the course of a decade, preservationists scraped, painted and patched the stone buildings flanking Main Street, then transformed them into picturesque and highly successful shops, inns and restaurants.

**William H. Schroeder House,
N62 W591 Washington Ave.**

Today, Cedarburg contains 104 buildings on the National Register of Historic Places and is graced with a downtown that looks almost as it did a century ago. It has paid a price for its preservation: Laden with specialty stores, art galleries and antique shops, Cedarburg can seem more like a tourist attraction than a regular little town. But there have also been benefits. Residents still have their beautiful buildings, and visitors enjoy not only good shopping but lovely architecture, too.

Look for the Cedarburg Woolen Mill (1865) at the intersection of Bridge Road and Washington Avenue; it is now the Cedar Creek Winery. The John Armbruster jewelry store (1910) at W62 N620 Washington Avenue, with its cast iron ornamentation and, inside, painted tin ceiling, is one of the few commercial buildings in Cedarburg still owned and operated by its founding family. The sidewalk clock is a rare cast iron clock that was made in Monessen, Pennsylvania, in the 1920s; the original one had been knocked down by a team of runaway horses. You'll find two of Cedarburg's historic inns nicely restored: The Central House Hotel (1853), now the Stagecoach Inn at W61 N520 Washington Avenue, and the Washington House Hotel (1886), at W62 N573 Washington Avenue. Still anchoring the town is the 1855 Cedarburg Mill, alongside Cedar Creek on Columbia Road. Five stories high and of Greek Revival design, it is considered one of the finest mills in the Midwest. It was executed in limestone, with lower walls 32 inches thick.

Chippewa Falls

An industrious community in the heart of the Chippewa River Valley

When the Wisconsin Territory was created in 1836, the Chippewa River Valley contained one-sixth of the pine timber west of the Appalachians. Chippewa Falls, like its neighbors Eau Claire and Menomonie, was part of a lumber boom that began in the 1840s in a region largely populated by French Canadian and Indian lumberjacks.

The first mill in Chippewa Falls was commissioned by the American Fur Trade Company in 1837. The townsite was platted in 1856 by developers envisioning a great milling center. An enormous new mill was built at the confluence of Duncan Creek and the Chippewa River in 1886. Known as the "Big Mill," it was reportedly the world's largest sawmill under one roof and capable of producing 400,000 board feet of lumber in 12 hours. Lumber remained the town's major industry into the early 1900s.

Downtown's commercial district lining Bridge St.

Chippewa Falls grew confidently; between 1860 and 1870 the population went from 674 to 2,507, a percentage increase seven times that of the entire state's growth. During the 1880s industry expanded to include flour mills, a brewery, and a woolen mill. When the lumber industry began its decline, enterprising townfolk invested in a variety of service and manufacturing industries, ensuring the town's survival.

Modern-day Chippewa Falls is a bustling community with a charming late-19th-century downtown. Selected as a Main Street Community in 1989, it earned a Great American Main Street Award in

Cardinal-Bergeron Building detail, 216 N. Bridge St.

(1889) at 101-105 Bridge Street, and the Union Block (1885) at 123 N. Bridge.

Around the corner from Bridge at 236 W. River Street stands the Sheeley House, which has housed a saloon business since 1884. The red brick building features ornate trim along the roofline and decorative window treatments in brick. Listed on the National Register of Historic Places, the Sheeley House is currently a restaurant and saloon.

One of the best preserved structures in the city is the Rutledge Charity Building (1916), 404 N. Bridge Street. This neoclassical building was built with funds from Edward Rutledge, local lumber magnate. The Rutledge family home (1873) at 505 W. Grand Avenue is not far from downtown, and it stands as testimony to the Rutledge fortune. The lavish two-story brick home features gingerbread trim, a cupola accented with a filigree of iron work, and veranda with extended portecochere. Built in 1873, the residence was sold in 1887 to Edward Rutledge, who remodeled it into the high Victorian Italianate structure you see today. Owned by the Chippewa County Historical Society, the Cook-Rutledge Mansion is open for tours during the summer.

1996. Downtown's center runs along Bridge Street, an extension of the Highway 53 bridge that crosses the Chippewa River. Note two commercial blocks on Bridge Street that stand out as excellent examples of renovation—the Metropolitan Block

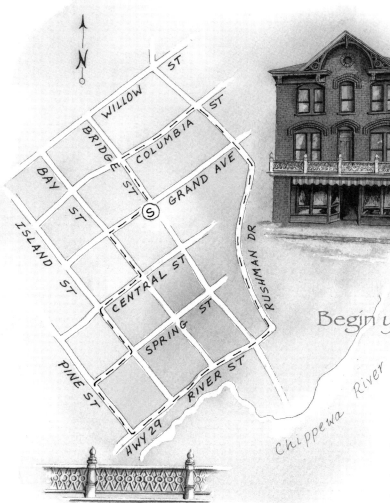

Begin your walk through the downtown area at the corner of Grand and Bridge. Walk west on Grand to Bay and turn left. Turn right on Central and then left on Island Street. Turn right on Spring Street, left on Pine and then left on River Street. Walk along River to the end, where it bends to the left and turns into Rushman. Walk up Rushman to Columbia and turn left, then left on Bridge and back to your starting point.

Be sure to include the Cook-Rutledge Mansion, 505 W. Grand, on your tour. You will want to drive west on Grand to the 500 block.

Cooksville

A hidden, sleepy village, and one of the state's
most architecturally significant communities

Everyone who visits Cooksville agrees: There is no other village in Wisconsin like it. No gas stations, no fast-food stores, no modern intrusions of any kind invade this secret spot off the main highway. Instead, around a New England-style "commons" stands a collection of well-preserved Greek and Gothic Revival residences, built in the mid-1800s. Nestled among trees and shrubbery, these diminutive homes lie like sleeping beauties: lovely, fragile and, seemingly, beyond the reach of time.

Cooksville was founded in 1840 when the families of John and Daniel Cook settled in an oak grove near Badfish Creek. In 1842, Dr. John Porter bought land near the Cooks from Senator Daniel Webster of Mas-

Bell tower and minarets, Congregational Church.

sachusetts, an early land speculator who had purchased the fertile acreage from the U.S. government. Porter deeded the "commons," or public square (an unusual feature in Wisconsin towns), to the village residents.

Early settlers, most of whom had come from New England, New York and the British Isles, grew wheat, and by 1850 Cooksville harbored 175 residents, a blacksmith shop, brickyard and opera house. When the wheat crop failed, farmers turned to dairying and tobacco. The Yankee settlers who moved farther west were replaced by industrious Norwegian immigrants. But when the railroad passed the little village by, Cooksville's future course was set. Without even a depot, it would remain forever a sleepy burg sur-

Begin your walk at the Cooksville Store on Main Street (Highway 138). Stroll south on Main Street past the Cook House until you reach the Congregational Church at the intersection of Main and Rock streets. Head east on Rock Street past lovely brick residences, then turn north on Webster Street. Turning right on Dane Street and right again, work your way around the commons to the old schoolhouse. If you are energetic, you can head east from here down Highway 59 and into the countryside. A mile and a half of walking takes you to Riley Road, a roller-coaster Rustic Road with sweeping views of lush farmland. Or retrace your steps back through Cooksville to your starting point.

rounded by fields and woods.

Cooksville did catch the discerning eye of preservationists, however, and today as you walk its few streets you will be charmed by their efforts. John Cook's house (1842) still stands on Main

General Store, in operation since the 1850s.

Street. On Webster Street, the Lovejoy-Duncan House (1848-1849) stands out with its square, stately contours and hip roof. The Longbourne House (1856) on Rock Street, made of local ver-

million brick with gingerbread barge boards, is equally striking. The Congregational Church on Main Street, with its elegant spires, has undergone extensive renovation. This was the village's first church; minister Jenkin Lloyd Jones, Frank Lloyd Wright's grandfather, preached at its dedication in 1879. Also standing is the village's schoolhouse (1886); the frame building with its distinctive bell tower is now the community center. Cooksville even retains a few retail operations: fittingly, a blacksmith shop and a general store. The latter, whose broad front porch still invites neighborly visits, has been in operation since 1847 —a year before Wisconsin became a state.

With 70 percent of its buildings built before the turn of the century, Cooksville is considered to be one of the state's most architecturally significant communities. You'll find this quaint gem of a village to be one of the most evocative, as well.

Eau Claire
Gateway city to northern Wisconsin

Located at the confluence of the Chippewa and Eau Claire rivers and at the southern edge of the pine-rich North Woods, Eau Claire developed into a major shipping point for lumber headed south. The first sawmills went up in 1845, and by 1890 more than 20 mills were operating in town—earning the town its nickname "Sawdust City." The lumber industry drew a steady stream of immigrant workers, who eventually settled three separate villages: one on the west bank of the Chippewa and two others on the north and south sides of the Eau Claire River. Bridges were eventually built across the rivers, joining the settlements, and the three were incorporated as the City of Eau Claire in 1872.

Millions upon millions of board feet of lumber have rolled out of the Eau Claire mills—between 1880 and 1885 these mills produced more than half of all the lumber manufactured in the Chippewa

Bailey House detail, 415 Gilbert Ave.

Valley. The successful lumber barons and merchants built enormous mansions with the fortunes they amassed. No details were spared, no indulgences denied. Decorative extravaganzas included wings and bays, parapets and turrets, complicated roof lines and elaborate shapes— the bigger the better.

By 1885, Eau Claire was the state's third largest city, with a population of 21,000, and it seemed the good life would never end. But the forests of the North Woods finally gave out, and by the 1890s the sawmills were closing. Eau Claire was lucky enough to make a successful transition to diversified manufacturing, and the surrounding area provided a strong agrarian base with dairy and wheat farming. The city embarked on a steady growth pattern, which continues today.

Eau Claire's heritage has been preserved in three historic districts within the city. A stroll through the Third Ward takes you through what was once the city's most prestigious residential neighborhood. Along these tree-lined streets, notably State Street, are the mansions built with seemingly limitless money and imagination.

The focal point of this neighborhood are four incredible Queen Annes located on Oakwood

Addison Cutter House, 1302 State St.

Place, a cul-de-sac off State Street. The Addison Cutter House, 1302 State Street, was constructed between 1885 and 1889. The exterior of this massive abode exhibits a variety of carvings, patterns, arcades, porches and cantilevered gables. Painted a warm gray with yellow, turquoise and lavender trim, the home is a true example of the opulence of the Victorian era. On the opposite corner, 1310

State Street, the David Drummond House (1888) is so large it almost defies belief. Constructed of brick and lumber, the home features innumerable porches, steep gables and multiple stories. A ballroom is located on the third floor.

The George Winslow House (1889) at 210 Oakwood Place was built from a plan purchased from a Tennessee architect. Though slightly smaller than its grandiose neighbors, it exhibits no shortage of decorative lavishness common to the Queen Anne style. The chimney rising up one side of the home is distinctive for its bricks gracefully framing a first-floor window. The William K. Galloway House (1888-89) is the fourth Oakwood Place residence at number 213. Built of brick, the three-story home features four extending gables and a tall chimney on the west side exhibiting recessed panels. This home also has a third floor ballroom.

Examples of working class homes come as a surprise among the extraordinary homes of the wealthy. The William Bailey House (1874), 415 Gilbert Avenue, is a good example of upright and wing/Italianate styling. Though now covered with shingles, it originally was covered in narrow wood clapboards. A small one-story Victorian cottage is found at 333 Summit Avenue and dates from 1881.

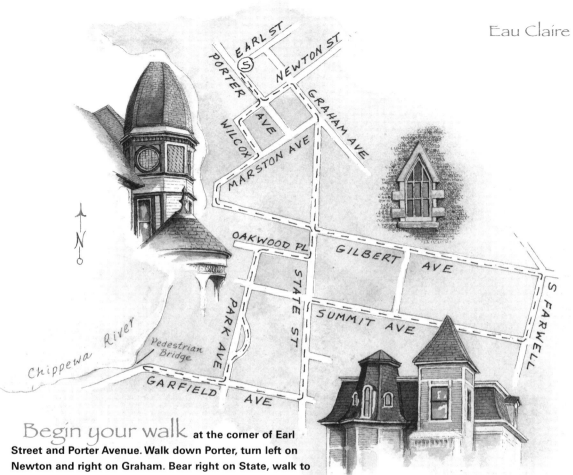

Eau Claire

Begin your walk at the corner of Earl
Street and Porter Avenue. Walk down Porter, turn left on
Newton and right on Graham. Bear right on State, walk to
Gilbert and turn left. Two blocks down, turn right on S. Farwell and then right on Summit until
you reach State again. Turn left on State, walk two blocks and turn right on Garfield. Walk through the
UW campus on Garfield to the river and the pedestrian bridge to gain a view of the Chippewa. Then
reverse your steps on Garfield to Park Avenue and turn left. Walk down Park and into Oakwood Place.
Turn right on Oakwood and come out on State, where you turn left. Turn left on Gilbert and follow it,
bearing right as Gilbert turns into Marston. Turn left on Wilcox, right on Newton, left on Porter and
you are back at your starting point.

Ephraim

A picturesque village on the shores of Green Bay

Ephraim is a pretty town. Its white clapboard-clad buildings and twin church spires inspire artists with their simple beauty, set as they are on the very edge of Green Bay. Look across the blue water of Eagle Harbor and you can spot sea caves in Peninsula State Park's Eagle Bluff. The lovely shorefront park provides a perfect place to enjoy ice cream from a local shop and watch the sun set. Founded by a religious congregation, and joined later by sturdy Norwegian immigrants whose culture still dominates the festivals of today, Ephraim has a rich cultural, historic and spiritual heritage.

Ephraim became home to Pastor Andreas M. Iverson and his Moravian congregation in 1853. They survived two bitter winters of near starvation

Village Hall detail, Highway 42.

when supply boats were frozen into Green Bay. Abraham Oneson's home (late 1800s) can still be seen at the corner of Highways 42 and Q. Abraham was one of the members of the scouting party that selected the site for the village in the winter of 1853. The Moravian Church (1859) was built a few years later, followed by the Lutheran Church in the early 1880s. Their twin steeples are landmarks for landlubbers and sailors alike, guarding the spiritual values of their founders. Even today, Ephraim is a "dry" town—no liquor sold here.

For many years, Ephraim was accessible only by water. Because of its visual charm, Ephraim attracted a lively tourist trade as early as the turn of the century. Many photographs from that era still exist and are on display in the

Begin your walk at the

Anderson barn on the corner of Highway 42 and Anderson Lane on the north end of town. Stroll down to the Anderson dock on the other side of Highway 42 and note the ice house and gas station. Be sure to visit the Anderson General Store if you find it open. Continue south on Highway 42 along the harbor and note the old hotels with fine broad verandas that face the water. Turn left on Moravia Street and climb the hill past the churches. The Pioneer Schoolhouse (1880) and the Goodletson Log Cabin (1857) at the top of the hill are open to the public and worth visiting. Enjoy the view of Eagle Harbor from the top of the bluff as you walk along. Turn left onto Cedar Street and go down the hill to Highway 42, turning right to retrace your steps to your starting place at the Anderson barn.

Anderson Hotel, Moravia St.

Anderson Lane from the barn now houses a gift shop. Across Highway 42 is the Anderson dock, warehouse (1858), and the general store (1858), which was the lifeline of the community until the early 1900s when roads were finally built between the towns. The warehouse, the third built on this site, once stored items for the general store and later held fish, crops, lumber and other farm products waiting for shipment by boat. Today the structure is covered with the signatures of boaters who have docked there. The general store was operated by the Anderson family for 100 years. It has since been beautifully restored as a museum and is open to the public in the summer months.

Turn-of-the-century hotels, ice cream parlors and general stores along Highway 42 catered to the already-active tourist trade of the early 1900s. The Hillside Hotel (1890) is the only "grand" hotel remaining from that period. Oscar Wilson's Confectionery and Ice Cream Parlor (1907), next to Hillside, is still in business. As you walk up Moravia Street to the top of the bluff you'll find the original schoolhouse and Goodletson log cabin. The cabin was moved to Ephraim from Eagle Island and originally housed seven people. Both buildings have been restored and are open to the public.

Anderson family barn (circa 1870). The barn was restored in 1990 as a museum and it houses the Ephraim Foundation, the organization responsible for the preservation of so many of Ephraim's historic buildings. Note the unusual square silo, one of only a few remaining in Door County.

The Anderson family left an indelible mark on Ephraim. The family home (1864) situated across

Evansville

Elegant Victorian residences, perfectly set on shaded streets

A Victorian air graces the streets of Evansville. Elaborate homes represent all the main architectural styles of the late 18th century: Greek Revival, High Victorian Gothic, Queen Anne, Italianate, Stick Style, Picturesque. If you love detail, you will find it here, in eyebrow windows, Ionic columns, gable roofs and scrolled brackets. Perhaps the most noticeable features, though, are Evansville's porches. You see them on almost every home in the historic district—a reminder of those relaxed Victorian summers when the evening's entertainment centered on reading the newspaper in a rocking chair and chatting with the neighbors who walked by.

In 1845, Evansville was known as the Grove because of its large stand of timber. Then, only a handful of log buildings constituted the town. When the first church—framed and painted—

Detail, Late Italianate, 224 W. Church St.

went up a year later, it was considered a very fine structure. More settlers came from western New York and Vermont. A religious group, they platted streets leading to a parklike square on which they built the Free Methodist Seminary. Today, their streetscape, the seminary, and the Yankee character all remain.

Economic development in Evansville was gradual but steady. On a main railroad line, it was, in the 1860s, the largest shipping point in the state for wool, and one of the largest shipping points for livestock. Other industries sprung up in response to the area's healthy farm trade: buttermaking, wagonmaking, windmill manufacturing and tobacco warehousing. Many believe that Evansville's fine architecture is a gift of this measured prosperity. Nineteenth-century residents did well enough to build nice homes, but lacking heavy urbanization, the town never had to be "renewed."

Main and Church streets showcase the most impressive houses. The Late Picturesque-style residence at 44 W. Main Street (1881) is a show-stopper, with a corner tower and projecting front bay.

Transitional Italianate, 100 College Dr.

The 1884 home of John Evans—first physician, first postmaster, first mayor and town namesake— is just down the street at 104 Main. At 143 W. Main (1879) you can still see a hitching post. This

home, a distinctive mustard color, also retains beautiful carpenter's detailing. At 228 W. Main (1874), an Italianate is a lovely teal and gold, with beautiful rope-beaded arched windows.

More handsome homes line Church Street, which parallels Main one block to the south. Look for the tall, rounded windows at 127 W. Church (owned by the same family from 1868 to 1976), and the iron cresting that adorns 113 W. Church (1880s). When you come to the Congregational Church (1863), First Baptist Church (1903), and Free Will Baptist Church (1854), you'll understand why this street was so named. By the way, the original bell for the latter was owned by all the town citizens who contributed the money for its purchase. It was used to call up the volunteer fire-fighting force.

The commercial district also has a few notable buildings. The Eager Free Public Library at 39 W. Main may be the finest of a series of libraries built by well-known Madison architects Claude and Starck. Designed in the Prairie style, it is listed on the National Register of Historic Places. And at 19-33 W. Main, the old Grange Store (1904) is an impressive landmark. When built it was the largest retail space in Wisconsin outside of Milwaukee.

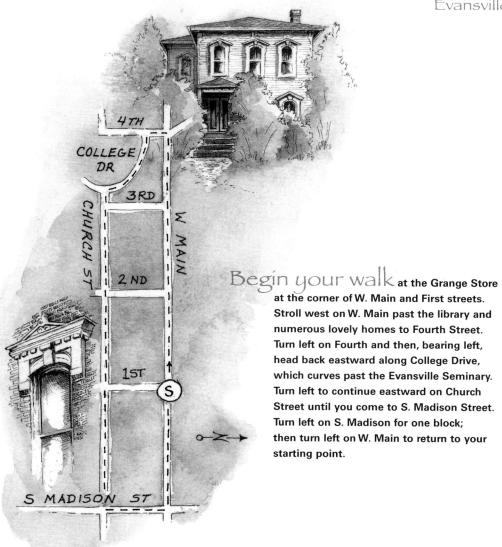

4TH

COLLEGE DR

3RD

CHURCH ST

W MAIN

2ND

1ST

S

S MADISON ST

Begin your walk at the Grange Store at the corner of W. Main and First streets. Stroll west on W. Main past the library and numerous lovely homes to Fourth Street. Turn left on Fourth and then, bearing left, head back eastward along College Drive, which curves past the Evansville Seminary. Turn left to continue eastward on Church Street until you come to S. Madison Street. Turn left on S. Madison for one block; then turn left on W. Main to return to your starting point.

Green Bay

A blue-collar town containing one of the state's most historic neighborhoods

The first European to step foot onto a Wisconsin shore, Jean Nicolet, did so in 1634 near Green Bay. Opportunistic fur traders soon followed, making "La Baye" an important outpost on the French-Canadian frontier. The British won control of the region in the 1760s, but it wasn't until 1816 that Americans gained a foothold with the establishment of Fort Howard on the west bank of the Fox River. Maps of this era show three communities within the area soon to be consolidated into Green Bay: Fort Howard, Navarino, and Astor.

Astor was originally part of a town platted by John Jacob Astor, founder of the American Fur Company. Though the area never became the town Astor envisioned, the district did become a prestigious residential neighborhood called Astor Heights, or The Hill. Some of the city's most prominent citizens built homes here during the

Italianate, front porch, 702 S. Monroe St.

late 19th and early 20th centuries when lumber and shipping replaced the fur trade and huge fortunes were to be made. Grand imposing homes—Queen Annes, Dutch Colonials, and Picturesque—were built along streets shaded by giant elms.

Today, these homes comprise the Astor Historic District. The 25-block area borders the Fox River on Green Bay's east side and was placed on the National Register of Historic Places in 1980. The focal point of the neighborhood is the resplendent mansion known as Hazelwood (1837) at 1008 S. Monroe Street. Built by Morgan Martin, the Greek Revival structure features columned verandas facing both the street and the river. Walk around to the back and midway down the lawn dropping to the river, then look back up at the home. The two black walnut trees marking this entrance lend evidence to the days when more visitors arrived via the Fox

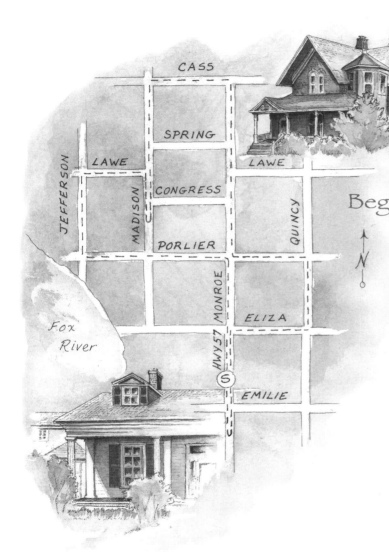

Begin your walk **at Hazelwood, 1008 S. Monroe Street, and head south to Emilie. Cross the street and walk back up Monroe to Eliza and turn right. Go to Quincy and turn left. Walk to Porlier and turn left, coming back to Monroe. Turn right on Monroe to Cass and turn left for one block. Turn left on Madison and head south, past Congress, then retrace your steps on Madison to Lawe. Turn left on Lawe, left on Jefferson, and left on Porlier. Walk two blocks on Porlier to Monroe, turn right and retrace your steps to Hazelwood.**

Note: The neighborhood around Hazelwood has restricted parking, though you can park on Monroe in front of Hazelwood in the summer. Be careful crossing Monroe (Highway 57) as it is a very busy street.

than the road. And Hazelwood surely hosted many visitors, for Martin was a well-known politician-president of Wisconsin's second constitutional congress—and it was in his dining room that Wisconsin's constitution was first drafted. The home is maintained as a historic site by the Neville Public

Georgian Revival, 903 S. Quincy St.

Museum, showcasing original furnishings, and it is open to the public Memorial Day to Labor Day.

Hazelwood sets the tone for an Astor walking tour. Its neighbors along Monroe range from the Neville residence (1890) an enormous Queen Anne at 905 S. Monroe, to an early Picturesque farmhouse-style home of red brick (circa 1870) at 645 S. Monroe. Traffic recedes and the river comes into view once you turn off Monroe. One of the loveliest spots on the walk is the stretch along Madison Street between Cass and Porlier. Here, homes surround a tree-shaded park covering an entire block, and a horse-drawn carriage would not seem out of place. The largest house in the Astor neighborhood is a lavender, pink, and blue Queen Anne (1898) at 736 S. Madison. The home features a three-story turret and a variety of surface textures. Many of the Queen Annes in this section have been painted in gay color schemes—even the subdued gray home at 804 S. Madison (1896) is trimmed in pink. The exterior of the home was influenced by the shingle style, and it features a variety of windows.

Back on Monroe, you find one of Green Bay's most impressive homes, The Elms, at 904 S. Monroe. Built between 1885 and 1889, The Elms exhibits a combination of Italianate and Queen Anne styles. It has been painstakingly restored over the past 20 years and today is clothed in its original colors. The elm trees that once surrounded the home are gone now, but a lovely English garden has replaced them.

Hudson

A border town located at the confluence of the St. Croix and Willow rivers

Hudson's roots reach back to Wisconsin's first years of statehood. Here, at the western edge of the state, early harvests of white pine from the North Woods were floated down the St. Croix River and through sawmills on the St. Croix and Willow rivers. Lumber formed the economic backbone of this river town and shaped its growth; the first generation of buildings were crafted from locally sawn white pine.

Settled first as a fur-trading outpost by a few French Canadians in 1840, Hudson's character was formed by the New England settlers who followed. It was they who built the sawmills and constructed the Greek Revival homes and white-steepled churches on the river bluffs. It was they who also named the town after the Hudson River in New York.

Lemuel North House, 903 Third St.

The first sawmill was built at the mouth of the Willow River in 1847, and its dam created Lake Mallalieu, which today separates Hudson and North Hudson. The heart of a busy milling district was located on the St. Croix at the southern end of town, called Sawmill Point, which today is the site of a marina. With the arrival of the railroad in 1871, Hudson's prosperity was assured.

Many mill towns sprang up along the state's rivers, but Hudson had an advantage over the rest: the town also served as an important crossing point to Minnesota. The first tow-rope ferry was established in the 1850s, which was pulled across the river by a driver and buggy for $1.00. Steam-powered ferries eventually replaced the tow rope, and then in 1913 the first interstate toll bridge was built across the St. Croix. In 1936 a lighted arch structure was put up at the Hudson entrance which illuminated the way for travelers until 1951, when the bridge was closed. The toll bridge no longer reaches the Minnesota shore, but the outskirts, however, leaving downtown and its immediate residential neighborhoods much as they were in the late 1800s, when a booming lumber industry supported the construction of a commercial district along Second Street and handsome homes along Third Street.

Philo Q. Boyden House, Victorian Gothic, 727 Third St.

Spooner House, 915 Third St.

the portion that remains is open to the public and is accessed from Lakefront Park.

With St. Paul, Minnesota, directly across the river, Hudson is one of the fasting growing towns in the state. This modern growth has been confined to

A fire in 1866 destroyed the early downtown; the sole survivor was the Star-Times Building, 112 Walnut Street, built in the 1860s. Downtown was quickly rebuilt, mostly with brick. Two banks went up in 1870: the National Savings Bank at 430

Begin your walk at the
intersection of Walnut and Third,
and stroll six blocks north along Third
to view Hudson's historic residential
district. Turn left at Myrtle, then left on
Second to walk through the commercial
district. When you reach Walnut turn
right to descend to the riverfront and
the entrance of Hudson's original bridge
to Minnesota. Turn around and walk
back up Walnut to Third and your
starting point.

MYRTLE ST

ORANGE ST

ELM ST

VINE ST

LOCUST ST

St Croix River

N

WALNUT ST

1ST ST

2ND ST

3RD ST

S

Octagonal Moffat-Hughes House, 1004 Third St., open for tours May-October.

Second Street and the First National Bank at 431 Second Street. In the next block, the Opera House (1880) is believed to be the only opera house still standing in the metro area of the Twin Cities. Now housing a restaurant and offices, the building has been restored to its original grandeur. A hotel was built next door in 1875 and became a center for prizefighting in the Midwest.

Hudson's prominent families built their homes along Third Street, one block above the commercial district and the St. Croix. The Darling-O'Brien home (1857), 617 Third, was erected by a pioneer Hudson contractor, Ammah Andrews. Take note of the Greek Revival's fine two-story portico—it is one of only a handful in the state. The Victorian Gothic mansion in the next block, 727 Third, was considered one of Hudson's mansions when it was constructed in 1879 for the enormous sum of $10,000. Exemplary of the elaborate residences along Third is the Lemuel North house (1884), 903 Third. This English Tudor was designed by St. Paul architect E.P. Bassford.

The centerpieces of the Third Street residences lie opposite each other in the 1000 block. The octagonal Moffat-Hughes house (1855), 1004 Third, is an excellent example of the novel eight-sided dwelling popular in the mid-1800s. This home, now a museum, was built by New Yorkers who had arrived in Hudson in 1854. Across the street at number 1005, the William Phipps house (1884) dominates the block. The size of this Italianate attests to Phipps' fortune, amassed in the lumber and railroad industries.

Janesville

A manufacturing city with an extraordinary collection of mansions

Janesville has a reputation as a hardworking city—with good reason. Manufacturing has long been its economic base, with General Motors and Parker Pen still prominent large employers. So you might expect the city to appear a bit scruffy, and certainly parts of it are. But Janesville also has pockets of loveliness, especially on Courthouse Hill, where the magnates who most profited from Janesville's industriousness once lived.

The town was founded in 1836 by Henry Janes, an enterprising and footloose character who operated the ferry, tavern, and post office, and platted a courthouse site for what the Territorial Legislature declared would be the county seat—before he moved west to the Pacific. The Rock River prompted Janesville's early industries: first the ferry and toll bridge, later a sawmill, flour mills and a woolen

Detail, 418 St. Lawrence Ave.

mill. The construction of three railroad lines propelled further growth. By the turn of the century, local manufacturers were producing machinery, carriages, barrels, shoes and fountain pens; the city was warehousing more than half of the state's tobacco crop; and 80 trains a day were pulling into its depots. Early in the 20th century, a local carriage company switched to automobile production. When General Motors opened its plant here in 1919, the wheels of industry rolled fast.

Fortunately, Janesville has preserved many of the structures that sprung up during its prosperous past. Of all state buildings listed on the National Register of Historic Places, about one-fifth are found here.

An extraordinary collection of mansions is situated on Courthouse Hill, a fine perch high above the Rock River. From their porches, balconies and cupolas, wealthy families no doubt enjoyed looking down not only on the river but also on the city they controlled. Strolling Courthouse Hill today, you find yourself wandering round and round the summit, enthralled by the elaborate architectural detailing and sheer size of these beautiful old residences.

Ornamental Queen Anne, 220 St. Lawrence Ave.

You'll likely notice first the Lovejoy house (1881)—now the YWCA—at 220 St. Lawrence Avenue. It was built by Allen P. Lovejoy after his marriage to Julia Stow; he was 55 and she 30. It's said that Lovejoy, a former carpenter, sat on a camp stool outside the house as it was being con-

structed to ensure that it was built to his specifications. During his lifetime, Lovejoy was president of the Harris Machine Company, a bank director, city mayor, and state senator. His wife established Janesville's first hospital and kindergarten and was active in the women's suffrage movement.

You'll find the 1878 home of Henry A. Doty, president of the Doty Box Company, at 209-211 S. Atwood Avenue. The Queen Anne at 118 Sinclair Street (1898) was built for Arthur J. Harris, the president of the Janesville Barb Wire Company. The imposing Georgian Revival at 625 St. Lawrence (1899), with its projecting bays and columned porch, once housed the president of the Merchants and Savings Bank. The very elegant Second Empire residence (1867) at 418 St. Lawrence—notice the beautiful entry and cast iron railings—was home to local crockery manufacturer Wadsworth G. Wheelock, and, later, bank president George Sutherland.

You'll also come upon three parks and a wooded gulley as you explore the neighborhood. All promote wonderful, broad views of the edifices that sit around them like distinguished matrons. One park, Upper Courthouse Park, has scarcely been altered since the time of settlement.

Begin your walk at the YWCA at 220 St. Lawrence Avenue.
From here, explore Courthouse Hill in a zigzag pattern: First take S. Division Street to
E. Holmes Street, turn left to S. Wisconsin Street, and left again back to St. Lawrence. Turning right,
head up St. Lawrence to Atwood Avenue and turn right to E. Holmes Street. Turn left and walk to
Jackman Street, then turn left back to St. Lawrence once again. Finally, walk up St. Lawrence one more
block to Sinclair Street, and turning right, follow it to its junction with E. Holmes. From here you can
choose a direct route back to your starting point via E. Holmes to S. Division Street, or take some time
to explore nearby streets in the neighborhood on which you will find additional impressive homes.

Kenosha

A community with a progressive past

As is true of Wisconsin's other manufacturing cities, Kenosha's image doesn't quite match reality. While it has its share of smoke-belching factories, there is considerable beauty as well. You'll find it in a cluster of lakefront parks and in a nice collection of historical buildings, many of which hold significant social import.

Settlers came to Kenosha in 1835, primarily to farm. Though situated on Lake Michigan, Kenosha never rivaled Milwaukee or Racine as a port —its harbor was less suitable for large freighters. In fact, the city remained small until after the Civil War, when a tannery and wagon factory began attracting workers. By the turn of the century, more than a hundred factories had taken hold and were offering employment to immigrants from Italy, Poland, Lithuania, Czecho-slovakia and Bohemia.

From its earliest years, Kenosha has been a progressive city noted for its public parks, literary magazines, labor movement and, at one time, socialist community. Just before the Civil War, the neighborhood around Library Park was active in the Underground Railroad. This neighborhood is still one of Kenosha's most interesting places to visit, with a fine collection of residential, religious, and civic buildings.

Detail, Urban J. Lewis House, 6019 7th Ave.

The library itself is glorious, designed in 1900 by architect Daniel H. Burnham, who was chief of construction for the 1893 World Columbian Exposition in Chicago. Be sure to go inside to admire the frescoed rotunda, marble floors, and inviting book-lined nooks. On the lawn before the library you'll find two statues also worth admiring: a

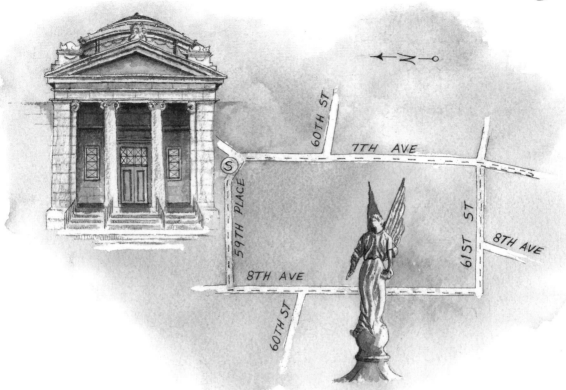

Begin your walk at the statue of Abraham Lincoln at the northeast corner of
Library Park. For a short walk, circle clockwise around the park. Proceed first down Seventh Avenue
to 61st Street (where a short sidetrip a few houses farther along Seventh takes you to Orson Welles'
birthplace). Then walk west on 61st Street to Eighth Avenue and north on Eighth Avenue to 59th
Place. A right turn onto 59th Place takes you back to your starting point. For a longer walk, you can
easily stroll to one or both of Kenosha's two other historic districts. The Civic Center District lies to
the northwest, roughly between 55th and 58th streets and Eighth and 11th avenues. The Third
Avenue District lies to the southeast along the lake between 61st and 66th streets.

Winged Victory designed by Burnham, and a bronze of Abraham Lincoln that is unusual for its relaxed pose. South of the Lincoln statue along Seventh Avenue is the original site of the home of

Edward Bain House, 6107 7th Ave.

Reverend Reuben Deming. His attic was one of four known "stations" in Kenosha that harbored fugitive slaves fleeing to freedom in Canada via ships on the Great Lakes.

The Urban J. Lewis house (1892), at 6019 Seventh Avenue, is bound to catch your eye. Very large and very pink, it is considered Kenosha's finest home in the Queen Anne style. The lovely Edward Bain house (1860) at 6107 Seventh Avenue was built for Edward Bain, whose wagon works became one of the most important industries in Kenosha and one of the largest wagonmaking factories in the state. A few doors down and across the street, the house at 6116 Seventh Avenue (1880) should be noted: Actor Orson Welles was born in the upstairs flat. It's said his first stage was the third-floor ballroom of the Frederick Gottfredsen house, around the corner at 711 62nd Street. You'll want to scrutinize the Gottfredsen house closely. Its owner worked first in his father's brewery and then took over a Kenosha branch of the Pabst Brewery. Imbedded in the stucco of the house's gable are pieces of beer bottles.

Also around the park stand the stately Masonic Temple (1924), Jewish Community Center (1927), First Church of Christ Scientist (1927), First Congregational Church (1874), the old YMCA (1930), and St. Matthew's Episcopal Church (1872). Tucked between them, at 6044 Eighth Avenue, is the tiny Volney French house (1846). Looking almost elfin among these imposing structures, it was the home of one of Kenosha's earliest settlers.

La Crosse

Founded by traders
on the bluffs of the Mississippi River

Located in the heart of the coulee region at the confluence of three rivers, the Black, the La Crosse, and the Mississippi, La Crosse is one of the most scenic towns in the state. Mark Twain referred to it as a "choice town" in *Life on the Mississippi* in 1896, and Wild Bill Cody liked it so much he brought his Wild West Show to town numerous times and eventually purchased land in the area.

Settlement of the town is credited to a New Yorker named Nathan Myrick who,

Storefronts along Pearl St.

at age 18, stepped off a riverboat on an island in the middle of the Mississippi and decided to stay. Myrick constructed a log cabin on what is today Pettibone Park and began trading with the local Ho-Chunk tribe. Despite a prime commercial location, La Crosse didn't realize a population boom until after statehood when an influx of German and Scandinavian immigrants arrived. From then on,

La Crosse thrived and grew. The railroad arrived in 1858; lumber from the North Woods floated down the La Crosse and Black rivers to the Mississippi; entrepreneurs became successful manufacturers and distributors of a variety of products; and enterprising German residents began brewing beer—making La Crosse for a time one of the state's brewing centers.

The downtown commercial historic district includes 110 buildings, most of them dating from the late 19th century. Powell Place, 200-212 Main, was built between 1872 and 1878. Italianate in style, this brick building features some elaborate details in the cornice, brackets and dentils. Farther down Main is the impressive Batavian Bank (1887-88), a five-story stone building. Cross the street to get a look at the top of the building and take note of the large rusticated arches on the facade. A prominent Chicago architect, Solomon

Beman, designed this fine example of Richardsonian Romanesque style. In the middle of the next block at 414 Main, the Rehfuss Building (1894) exhibits an eclectic mix of Romanesque, Queen Anne and neoclassical styles. A close look reveals elabo-

Batavian Bank Building, 319 Main St.

rate window surrounds and an ornate cornice.

A block over, you find La Crosse's oldest commercial buildings in the 200 block of Pearl Street. The Vogel Building (1866), 213-215 Pearl, is constructed of local brick. Its Vernacular style is a bit plainer than its neighbor, the Zeisler Building (1886), 201 Pearl. The Zeisler was constructed for local brewmaster George Zeisler in the Italianate

style. Note the pediment near the roof line and the cornice. The specialty shops that fill these storefronts today add to the charm of this section of your walk. Take time to stop in at the old-fashioned ice cream parlor for a phosphate or ice cream soda.

What was once the Pamperin Cigar Company (1879) faces the river on Second Street. The brick Italianate building exhibits an elaborate metal cornice with brackets, dentil trim, and ornamental window hoods. Until 1942 cigars were hand-made here and shipped nationwide.

Though not on the official walking tour, a few more stops should be made while you are in town. The Freight House Restaurant, 107 Vine, is located in a former Chicago-Milwaukee-St. Paul Railroad warehouse. The restaurant features soaring brick archways and plenty of railroad memorabilia. Down on the waterfront, Riverside Park offers a peaceful view of the Mississippi as well as a chance to see the paddlewheel tour boats. At the far end of the park, a 25-foot sculpture of Hiawatha, a Native American brave, stands at the meeting point of the three rivers. And at 111 Third Street stands the world's largest six-pack, home of the G. Heileman Brewery, open for tours.

Begin your walk at the corner of Main
and Second streets. Walk away from the river to Third
Street and turn left. Walk one block to State and turn right.
Turn right on Fourth, and in the middle of the block cut
through the parking lot to Fifth Avenue. Turn right on Fifth
and right on Main for one block. Turn left on Fourth and
walk to Pearl. Turn right on Pearl, walk two blocks to
Second and turn right, back to Main and your starting point.

Lake Geneva
A Victorian resort in a beautiful lake setting

The town of Lake Geneva is like a jewel dropped in a cornfield. Small, surrounded by the agricultural lands of southeast Wisconsin, it could easily be overlooked. But its clear, blue, spring-fed lake is so lovely and the mansions that surround it so stunning, that the locale attracts visitors as strongly as a sparkling diamond—just as it has for more than a century.

The area began developing as a tourist destination in the 1860s after the Chicago North Western Railroad brought a line here from Chicago, just 75 miles away. By 1879, Lake Geneva was the summer home of the rich and powerful. Ten trains a day pulled in, plus a weekend service known as the Millionaire's Special for the company presidents who ensconced their families here for the season, arrived themselves on Friday night, and returned to their Chicago offices Monday morning. By 1910, all the lakeshore property,

**Riviera Concourse
on the lakefront.**

GENEVA LAKE AREA CHAMBER

with the exception of a few public beaches, was transformed into private resorts and estates.

The summer "homes" were, in reality, palaces. Multistoried, with generous porches, turrets, and elaborate stonework, and surrounded by lush gardens and carefully landscaped lawns, they rimmed Geneva Lake like pearls on an exquisite, expensive necklace. Their owners—Wrigley, Swift, Maytag, Crane and Drake, among others—named them fancifully: Maple Lawn, Fair Field, Gay Lynne, Bonnie Brae, Folly, Tyrawley, Loramoor. One owner, R.R. Chandler, bought a reproduction of a Buddhist temple that had been the Ceylon government's exhibit at the 1893 Columbian Exposition and transported it to Lake Geneva. He built an elaborate addition, constructed a feudal-style tunnel that connected its basement to the water's edge, and then then moved in. Old photographs depict the scene: thoroughbred horses in the pad-

Begin your walk at the Riviera Concourse. To arrange a pick-up at Williams Bay, first stop by the ticket office of the Lake Geneva Cruise Line. From here, walk counter-clockwise around the lake. You'll cross the beach in front of the public library first; then the route narrows to a path. Follow the path, which is unmarked but easy to follow, until you reach Williams Bay Lakefront Park, a distance of about seven miles.

docks, tea parties in the gazebos, parasoled ladies strolling the paths, and steam-driven yachts cruising the lake.

The gentle Victorian ambiance is long gone, of course. But Lake Geneva's beautiful setting remains, as do many of the spectacular mansions.

Private resorts and estates line Geneva Lake.

The most pleasant way to take in the scenery is on foot. Town law requires Lake Geneva landowners to maintain three feet of public access around the lake's perimeter. The result is a 26-mile-long Shore Path that traverses the lawns of all the elegant places, giving walkers a unique, intimate view of this exceptional community. (The path itself is a fascinating mix of building materials and a testa-

ment to the range of the human imagination.) It takes about nine hours to walk the entire path, but shorter segments are possible, either by heading out and returning by retracing your route, by arranging a car shuttle, or by hopping aboard the Geneva Lake cruise boat to get back to your starting point.

Between Lake Geneva and Williams Bay, you encounter the Riviera Concourse (1932), an elegant structure in which Tommy Dorsey and Louis Armstrong once played. Nearby is the Lake Geneva Public Library (1954), a Prairie-style building designed by a student of Frank Lloyd Wrights. (Step inside to enjoy the restful view from the reading room's broad windows.) Farther along the path, the Wrigley Estate ("Green Gables") is distinguished by white homes with green-painted roofs and trim. Villa Hortensia (1906), a large white stucco home with a red tile roof and matching birdhouses, was built for E.F. Swift, son of the founder of the Swift meatpacking company. This section of path also treats you with a nice view of the Yerkes Observatory (1897). Owned by the University of Chicago, it houses the world's largest refracting telescope and is graced with lovely architectural detail.

Madison
Mansion Hill Historic District
A showcase for the 19th-century social and business elite

Also known as Yankee Hill, Aristocrat Hill and Big Bug Hill, the Mansion Hill Historic District was settled by Madison's upper class in the mid-19th century. Large, ornate residences with elaborate details were built on a wooded hill on the shores of Lake Mendota just north of the state capitol.

In 1848, Wisconsin became the 30th state and the capital city also was selected as the site for the new state university. Many of Madison's

Detail of stone stair, Gorham St.

buildings were built in the boom decade after statehood, and in response to the needs of the university. The popular architectural styles of the day were represented: Queen Annes sprang up next to German Romanesque Revival and Italianate mansions to house students, faculty members, politicians, and bankers.

One of the earliest German Romanesque Re-

vival structures, The Gates of Heaven Synagogue (1863), was the first synagogue in Madison, and today is one of the oldest surviving synagogues in the nation. Originally situated on W. Washington Avenue, the synagogue was saved from demolition and moved to its present location in James Madison Park on the lakefront. Built of sandstone and brick, the building shows the strong influence of contemporary German design on architect August Kutzbock (1814-68) and is considered an example of his finest work.

The Old Governor's Residence (1856) at 130 E. Gilman Street served as the executive residence for 17 Wisconsin governors from 1885 to 1950. The home was built of locally quarried sandstone in the Italianate style. Also note the restored Queen Anne across the street at 125 E. Gilman. Its curved porch would have provided a good location from which to enjoy the cool breezes off the lake—and it is just as inviting today.

As you continue along Gilman Street, you come upon four elegant mansions on the corners of Gilman and Pinkney streets. The sandstone Kendall

Keenan House, 28 E. Gilman St.

house (1855) at 104 E. Gilman was the first of the four to be built. Its Italianate style was modernized in 1873 when its French Second Empire mansard roof was added. The Keenan house (1857) at 28 E. Gilman is spectacular. The German Romanesque Revival design features a stone balcony railing over the double front doors and ornate ironwork along the roofline and cupola.

Across the street at 424 N. Pinckney the Mc-

Donnell/Pierce house (1857-58) may well be the finest example of the German Romanesque Revival remaining in the United States. Now restored and run as the Mansion Hill Inn, it has decorative stonework resembling that of the second capitol, which was built by the same contractor. Exquisite ironwork decorates the covered front door and trims the many balconies.

Although the lake is not on the walking tour, you can turn right on Wisconsin Avenue to take in the view of Lake Mendota and admire the Queen Anne and Early Empire homes along the way. Then backtrack to Gilman and cross Wisconsin Avenue to continue your tour. In the next block at 14 W. Gilman (circa 1880) you'll see the house where Thorton Wilder was born. In the early 1860s, John Muir was a frequent guest at the White House (1856) at 114 W. Gilman, home of Prof. Ezra Carr and his wife, Jane.

At 120 W. Gorham, the Wootton-Mead house (1907) is a fine example of the Prairie style. Notice the bands of the leaded glass windows and strong horizontal lines. Be sure to stop at the tiny Period Garden Park to rest during your walk and admire the Keyes house (1853) at 102 E. Gorham, a rambling brick Italianate house.

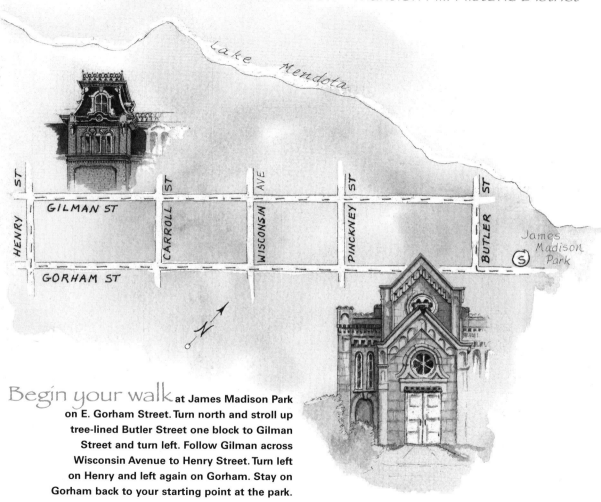

Begin your walk **at James Madison Park on E. Gorham Street. Turn north and stroll up tree-lined Butler Street one block to Gilman Street and turn left. Follow Gilman across Wisconsin Avenue to Henry Street. Turn left on Henry and left again on Gorham. Stay on Gorham back to your starting point at the park.**

Madison
Third Lake Ridge
An eclectic mix of homes

Located on a glacial drumlin on the north shore of Lake Monona, Madison's Third Lake Ridge Historic District encompasses architectural styles as diverse as its earliest residents. Bankers and plumbers, factory owners and tailors shared the neighborhood and built homes reflecting their tastes and pocketbooks. The current residents have shown an interest in renovation, although many of the original buildings have been lost and some are in need of restoration. The district currently has nine buildings listed on the National Register of Historic Places, and 13 have been designated as Madison Landmarks.

Most of Third Lake Ridge was developed by Leonard J. Farwell (1819-89), a New York native who purchased most of the land east of the square in 1847. Farwell built an impressive three-story sandstone octagon on the highest point of the ridge for his residence, completed in 1855. He became the leading resident of the district and was soon joined by other Yankee

**Commanding a view
of Lake Monona.**

businessmen who built their homes on the ridge. Although most of these homes have been demolished, the Shipley-Suttleworth house (1855) at 946 Spaight Street has been preserved. One of the oldest surviving buildings in the district, it is constructed of narrow-gauge, soft red brick in a combination of Greek Revival and Italianate styles. The John T. and Harriet Martin house (1855) at 1033 Spaight Street is another early neighborhood home. Tucked between modern buildings, the Martin house is a reasonably intact example of a high-styled Italianate residence. Notice the broad frieze under the eaves,

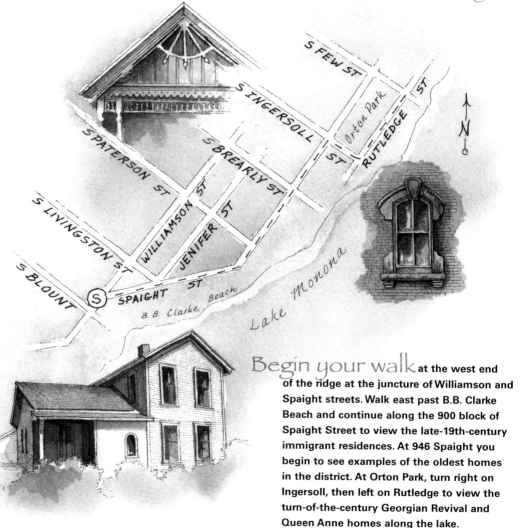

Begin your walk at the west end
of the ridge at the juncture of Williamson and
Spaight streets. Walk east past B.B. Clarke
Beach and continue along the 900 block of
Spaight Street to view the late-19th-century
immigrant residences. At 946 Spaight you
begin to see examples of the oldest homes
in the district. At Orton Park, turn right on
Ingersoll, then left on Rutledge to view the
turn-of-the-century Georgian Revival and
Queen Anne homes along the lake.

and the narrow attic windows, paneling and paired brackets.

John George and Lucia Ott House, 754 Jenifer St.

After the Civil War, the Third Lake Ridge housed a growing number of immigrants at its western edge. Swiss and German businessmen built handsome brick homes in the 700 block of Jenifer Street, while less prosperous immigrants built frame cottages. The John Kircher house (circa 1877) at 733 Jenifer, built in a high Victorian-Italianate style, features carved sandstone hood moldings and oculus (round window). Across the street is the Adolph and Mary Klose house (circa 1870), consisting of a two-story block with a one-story ell. This ell-plan design is typical of the immigrant housing popular in the late 19th century.

The east end of the district contains mostly turn-of-the-century residences. The Curtis house (1901) at 1102 Spaight is an attractive, well-preserved Queen Anne. Most noteworthy are its curved porch, diamond-paned Palladian windows, and corner tower. Perched on the corner of Spaight and Ingersoll streets, it has a nice view of Orton Park. Originally, the park was the village cemetery, but all the remains had been moved to Forest Hill Cemetery by 1877, and thus Orton Park became Madison's first public park.

Continuing on, an excellent example of Prairie School architecture can be found at 620 S. Ingersoll in the Lougee house (1907), which has lovely leaded windows. The George P. and Annie Miller house (1907) at 1125 Rutledge is an attractive and impressive Georgian Revival house of red brick trimmed with limestone.

Milwaukee
Third Ward
City of immigrant neighborhoods

Milwaukee's landscape was originally defined by three rivers—the Kinnickinnic, the Milwaukee, and the Menomonee—running together in a marshland edged by Lake Michigan. Full of wildlife and stretches of wild rice, this area was home to a number of Native American tribes. (The name "Milwaukee" is believed to mean "good land" in Menominee or Potawatomi.) French fur traders visited this area during the 18th century but preferred to operate out of Green Bay. Thus, Milwaukee did not become a "settlement" until two fur traders, Solomon Juneau and Jacques Vieau, set up camp in the region in the 1820s.

When the Menomineee, Potawatomi, Fox and Sauk tribes ceded the southeastern portion of

Gargoyle, Baumbach Building, 312 E. Buffalo St.

Wisconsin to the United States in 1831, the region was open to settlers and speculators. Three settlements were established by the time the dust settled: Juneautown on the east bank of the Milwaukee River, Kilbourntown on its west bank, and Walker's Point to the south where the Menomonee and Milwaukee flow into Lake Michigan. Competition was fierce between the three villages, but by 1846 they were unified as the City of Milwaukee. The original boundaries of the villages are evident today by the bridges that cross the rivers at odd angles because the three towns couldn't agree on how to align the streets.

The city's population virtually exploded between 1840 and 1880 with an influx of immigrants, and Milwaukee quickly became a city of neighborhoods defined by ethnic origin. Among the first groups to arrive were the Irish, who settled in the Third Ward because of the area's proximity to unskilled labor opportunities: construc-

bounded by St. Paul Avenue on the north and Milwaukee Street on the east.

Two major tragedies eventually drove the Irish from the Third Ward. In 1860 an excursion ship

The 200 block of North Water Street.

tion sites, wharves, and the railroad. It was also close enough to the mansions of Yankee Hill, enabling the young women to walk to work as domestics. The Third Ward's boundaries were Wisconsin Avenue to the north, Lake Michigan to the east, and the Milwaukee River to the west and south. Today's historic Third Ward is much smaller,

from Chicago went down in Lake Michigan, losing more than 300 passengers, most of whom were Third Ward residents. Then in October 1892, the worst fire in Milwaukee's history leveled more than 440 buildings in a 16-block area of the Ward, leaving more than 2,000 residents homeless. Rebuilding began almost immediately, but the dis-

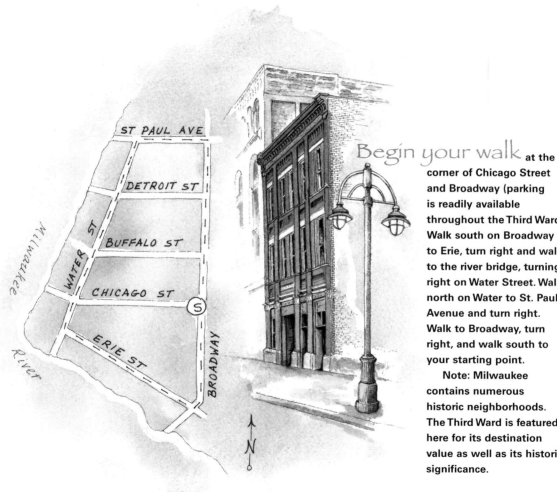

Begin your walk **at the corner of Chicago Street and Broadway (parking is readily available throughout the Third Ward). Walk south on Broadway to Erie, turn right and walk to the river bridge, turning right on Water Street. Walk north on Water to St. Paul Avenue and turn right. Walk to Broadway, turn right, and walk south to your starting point.**

Note: Milwaukee contains numerous historic neighborhoods. The Third Ward is featured here for its destination value as well as its historic significance.

heartened Irish left and Italians moved in. By 1915 the neighborhood housed 45 groceries, 29 saloons, two spaghetti factories and a bank, all owned by Italians. By 1919 the Third Ward's wholesale trade was the largest business activity in Milwaukee.

Pabst Saloon, 124-6 N. Water St.

By 1957, the Third Ward's gradual transition from a commercial/residential area to a solely commercial area had been completed with the demolition of the small frame homes in the neighborhood. New one-story and low-rise factories were built during the 1960s, but the majority of the remaining buildings in the Ward were built between the late 1890s and the 1920s. As a result, some consider the Third Ward to be one of the best indigenous warehouse districts in the country.

It is also a district designed by the leading local architects of the day. You find buildings in a variety of styles, including Renaissance Revival (Cawker Estate Building, 200-208 N. Water), Victorian Gothic (Jewett & Sherman Company, 343 N. Broadway), Romanesque Revival (Phoenix Knitting Works, 311 E. Chicago), Queen Anne (Engine Company No. 10, 176 N. Broadway), and Victorian (Ryder Building, 181 N. Broadway). Close examination of the buildings reveals decorative touches true to the individual styles. Take note of the elaborate carvings on the Baumbach Building, 312 E. Buffalo.

Named to the National Register of Historic Places in 1984, the Third Ward today has experienced a renaissance. Wholesale trade is still active in the 300 block of Broadway known as Commission Row, but the newest immigrants to the Ward include art galleries, specialty shops, cafes, lofts and condos. With a pedestrian mall on Broadway, a small park, and tasteful street lighting, this is once again a neighborhood full of life.

Mineral Point

The point of Wisconsin's beginnings

White settlers first began to trickle into southwestern Wisconsin—then an unremarkable corner of the vast Michigan Territory—in the early 1800s. Many of these newcomers were miners, wandering the hills with divining rods in search of lead, called "mineral" in those days. When "mineral" was discovered in the rocky ridgetops of a steep-sided valley, a camp was established and christened Mineral Point. One of the first successful miners was Henry Dodge, who arrived in 1827 and within a year was hauling a ton of ore out of the ground daily. By the 1830s Mineral Point was a bona fide boom town, and it was here that the Territory of Wisconsin was created on July 4, 1836, with the inauguration of Dodge as the first governor.

When word of the land's riches reached hard-

Stone cottage window.

rock miners in Cornwall, England, several hundred came to Mineral Point, settling in the shadow of the Merry Christmas Mine hill. The Cornish—skilled stonecutters and masons—utilized the local limestone to build neat rows of small stone cottages like those they had left behind. Their neighborhood was quickly dubbed "Shake Rag Under the Hill," because a miner's wife would summon her husband home for dinner by shaking a rag out the window or door.

Zinc mining replaced lead mining in the 1860s and carried the town until the Great Depression, when zinc prices collapsed and in 1932 the town's only bank failed. The little cottages of the stone miners stood empty and crumbling, the downtown quiet and dusty.

But Mineral Point was lucky to experience a

renaissance, beginning with the restoration of a cottage and row house, Pendarvis, on Shake Rag Street in the late 1930s, and continuing with an influx of artists renovating storefronts for studios and shops in the following years. In 1970 the Wis-

and across the street walking trails criss-cross the hillside where the Merry Christmas Mine was located. More limestone houses stand at the end of Shake Rag Street, at the intersection of Commerce Street and Highways 39 and 23. Follow the path

High Street, looking toward Commercial St. **Jail Alley.**

consin State Historical Society purchased Pendarvis to operate as a museum. In 1971, the downtown was listed as Wisconsin's first historic district on the National Register of Historic Places.

The Cornish heritage is meticulously maintained along Shake Rag Street, the oldest section of Mineral Point. The historical site, Pendarvis, includes a series of restored stone and log cottages,

between the buildings on your right to the stone potter's barn, built in the 1850s.

Commerce Street was the center of the original commercial district; 209 Commerce (1838-39) is the earliest structure remaining in this area. The storefronts along this stretch are typical of the early stone architecture of the region: front elevations of dressed stone with side walls of rough

Begin your walk at the historic site, Pendarvis, on Shake Rag Street. Head south on Shake Rag, cross the highway intersection, and continue south on Commerce Street. Walk as far as the railroad depot and the "mineral point," then reverse direction and walk back up Commerce to Jail Alley. Turn left on Jail Alley, walk up the hill to Chestnut, and turn left. Walk to High Street and turn right to climb the hill to the top (Green Lantern Antiques). Backtrack down High Street to the bottom, turn left on Commerce, and retrace your steps back to Pendarvis on Shake Rag Street.

stone, punctuated by plain windows with flat stone lintels. At the bottom of Commerce you will find the Mineral Point Depot (1857), built of native limestone and believed to be the oldest depot in

Row Houses, Pendarvis.

the state. The ridge of land rising up to the east marks the spot where lead was first discovered— the "mineral point." The Walker House, a block over, is the oldest standing hotel in town, built between 1836 and 1860. The Chesterfield Inn, across Commerce, was a stagecoach stop, and it still houses travelers behind its foot-thick walls.

Look closely at the bluff behind the inn to see "badger holes," small caves lived in by the miners before they built their homes.

The streets heading up the hill from Commerce twist and turn, following the footpaths of miners. Halfway up Jail Alley, so named because the log jail was located here at the back of the courthouse, stands a lovely brick home, built between 1846 and 1847 by Parley Eaton, the first judge of Iowa County. Eaton had come from Massachusetts, and the home's clean federal lines and crow-step gables reflect a style popular on the East Coast. The salmon-red bricks were made from clays found in the area and fired in a local brickyard.

A walk to the top of High Street, the center of the retail district, provides a panoramic view of the historic storefronts descending the steep hill. Crafted from brick and stone from the 1850s to about 1900, the majority of the commercial buildings reflect the vernacular stone construction popular during this period. A few examples of Queen Anne style are evident, with towers and bays, decorative shingles, and a metal front (229 High Street). The result is a downtown that looks remarkably similar to the sepia-toned photos displayed in many of the shops.

70

Platteville

Walk in the footsteps of the lead miners up and down narrow, hilly streets

As you stroll the streets of Platteville, you can't help but be aware of the streets themselves. They go uphill and downhill. They zig and they zag. Sometimes they stop abruptly, seemingly for no reason. But there is a reason—or there was one for this complex pattern. In the early part of the 19th century, Platteville was pocked with lead mines. When town surveyors laid out the streets, they had to respect the miners' property rights, which meant their sometimes going around or stopping dead when they came to a shaft. In other cases, the surveyors simply

Mining equipment display, Mining Museum.

followed the paths the miners had already worn into the ground. Walk Platteville today, and your steps literally trace this town's history.

The first white man to discover lead here—in an animal den in a stream bank—was trapper Emanuel Metcalf. In 1827, Major John H. Rountree and James B. Campbell bought Metcalf's claim. The Rountree Lode was a rich one, producing more than 5 million pounds of ore before the mineral ran out, making Rountree the town's most prominent citizen. At the height of the lead boom, Platteville was the region's hub, filled with hard-working men out to make a fortune. It was also home to the nation's first mining school; thus, the mammoth "M" that sits upon Platteville Mound east of town.

Though the land underneath Platteville is honeycombed with mine shafts, only one is accessible today: Bevan's mine, dug in 1844. Rediscovered in 1972 through exploratory drilling, it was restored by the citizens of Platteville and now is part of a small museum complex. The rest of the town holds an interesting mix of historic old architecture (including a small but charming downtown) interspersed with modern homes. It all sits exposed on the hills of the scenic, unglaciated southwest, mine shaft itself. Nearby residential streets contain a few early homes, including the S.O. Paine house (1862) at 155 Water Street, built for one of Platteville's first lawyers; and the Edward Davies house (circa 1860) at 315 N. Second Street.

Edward Davies House, 315 N. 2nd St.

Rountree House.

whipped by a wind that blows relentlessly, like the passage of time itself.

The Mining Museum is the best place to begin a visit to Platteville. Not only can you look at displays telling the story of mining in southwest Wisconsin, but you can actually descend into the

After walking though Indian Park—an unmarked cemetery in which cholera victims were buried—you'll come to a collection of more elaborate historic homes. The Mitchell-Rountree stone cottage (1837), built of local limestone by Rev. Samuel Mitchell, sits in a lovely grove of trees at

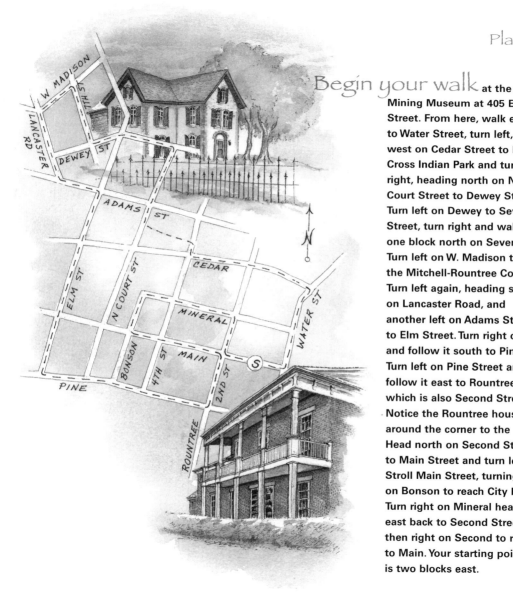

Begin your walk **at the Mining Museum at 405 E. Main Street. From here, walk east to Water Street, turn left, walk west on Cedar Street to Fourth. Cross Indian Park and turn right, heading north on N. Court Street to Dewey Street. Turn left on Dewey to Seventh Street, turn right and walk one block north on Seventh. Turn left on W. Madison to the Mitchell-Rountree Cottage. Turn left again, heading south on Lancaster Road, and another left on Adams Street to Elm Street. Turn right on Elm and follow it south to Pine. Turn left on Pine Street and follow it east to Rountree, which is also Second Street. Notice the Rountree house around the corner to the right. Head north on Second Street to Main Street and turn left. Stroll Main Street, turning right on Bonson to reach City Park. Turn right on Mineral heading east back to Second Street, then right on Second to return to Main. Your starting point is two blocks east.**

the intersection of Madison and Lancaster streets. The Reverand's daughter married town founder John Rountree; the cottage contains original furnishings, and is occasionally open to the public.

Mitchell-Rountree Stone Cottage.

Adjacent to each other at 440 and 390 W. Adams Street are the Jonathan H. Evans house (1870) and the Captain Beebe house, built for prominent early citizens. (Notice the intricate wrought iron on the Evans residence.) A string of buildings on Elm

Street also catches the eye: the imposing Rountree Hall (1853), originally the Platteville Academy and later the state's first teacher training college; the Eastlake-style Schoolmaster's House (1852) at 65 N. Elm, built for the Platteville Academy's headmaster; and the turreted Burg house (1906) at the corner of Elm and Main. The latter has 18 rooms, including one on the third floor that was devoted exclusively to the Burg family's cats. John Rountree's house (1854) is at the intersection of Rountree and Pine. Since Rountree's family was from Virginia, this building resembles a plantation home, with a generous verandah onto which floor-to-ceiling windows open.

On Main Street, you see a number of gracefully aging commercial buildings, many constructed of the local brick, which is a particularly warm, rich red. The nearby City Park was once the public square, full of mud and riddled with mine shafts. One of the largest mines entered the ground at the site where the Carnegie Library (1915) now stands. Be sure to look for a small, leaning building three short blocks away on the northwest corner of Mineral and Second streets—this is the former stopping point for the stagecoach line that linked Platteville to Galena and Madison.

Plymouth

A charming New England town

Historic Plymouth lies in the Mullet River Valley, ringed by wooded hills and immaculate dairy farms on the northeastern edge of the Kettle Moraine. The town owes its origins to Henry Davidson, a savvy entrepreneur who early realized the profit to be made from traffic along the wooden plank road between Sheboygan and Fond du Lac. Davidson, together with his son, Thomas, laid claim to a spot in the wilderness midway along the road's projected route, and put up a tavern and inn in 1845. Their establishment, Cold Springs Tavern, did a brisk business, and Plymouth soon became more than a stop on the way to somewhere else.

Davidson also had a hand in establishing Plymouth as an agricultural and manufacturing center by opening saw and flour mills along the nearby Mullet River in 1848 and 1850. Yankees from New York and New England arrived and stayed,

St. Paul's Episcopal Church, 312 E. Main St.

followed by German immigrants. By the 1870s, Plymouth was gaining a reputation as "Cheese Capital of the World" with the creation of the Plymouth Dairy Board of Trade (now the National Cheese Exchange in Green Bay). Prosperous mill owners and merchants built their homes on "Yankee Hill" high above the river, while the commercial district, developed between 1880 and 1910, lined the riverbanks below.

Today, a stroll through downtown reflects this late-19th-century prosperity in carefully maintained brick buildings, especially lining Mill Street. The "queen" of these structures is the Laack Block on the corner of Mill and Stafford streets. Built by H.C. Laack between 1889 and 1898, this corner building presents a medieval appearance, with numerous chimneys and parapets defining its roofline. A mortar and pestle crown the Adams Pharmacy, evidence that the building traditionally housed a drug store. It also housed the Laack Hotel (1892) on the side street, 52 Stafford, built as an extension of the Laack Block. The hotel is a grand example of Queen Anne elegance, with double bays and dormers surrounding a portico entrance, painted white with Celtic green trim. Completely

Dow House, 425 Collins St.

renovated in 1986, the hotel is now an elegant Irish inn named 52 Stafford and is listed on the National Register of Historic Places.

Across the river on Collins Street, Plymouth's elite built imposing residences on Yankee Hill, commanding a view of the surrounding countryside as well as the bustling downtown. These were the homes of bankers, mill owners, and successful merchants, built in a variety of styles ranging from Italianate to Greek Revival to Queen Anne. The mansions sit well back from the road, graced by huge trees and well-kept gardens. At the eastern end of the street, 405 Collins (1870-71), sits the only residence in Plymouth to be listed on the National Register of Historic Places. The home was designed by Andrew Jackson Downing for Henry Huson in the Gothic Italianate style. Though the home had many early additions, the board and batten siding has remained unchanged over the years, and the present color scheme is representative of 1885 colors. The muted color almost hides the house among the tree-filled yard. Directly across the street is the water tower Huson had constructed in 1885 to provide running water to his home. The tower originally included a windmill, enabling water to be pumped across the street to the house, stored in reservoirs on the second floor, and released to the first floor by gravity.

Another Huson, Gilbert, built the lovely Queen Anne next door (1891). In contrast to its neighbor, this home sits in an open yard, crowning the last spot on Collins before the street dips down to the railroad depots and downtown. The home retains many original features and fine detailing.

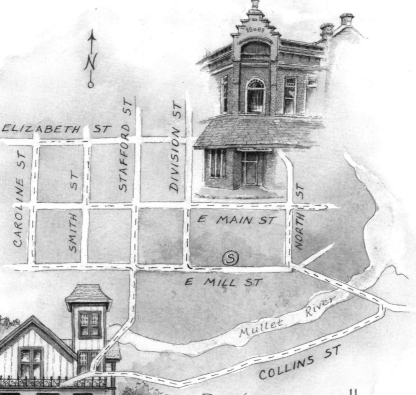

Begin your walk at the Plymouth Center,
520 E. Mill Street. Head west on Mill, turn right on Division, then right
on E. Main to North Street. Cross North, continuing on E. Main to the
B.L. Nutt house at 632 E. Main, then retrace your steps to North Street.
Turn left on North, cross E. Mill, and climb up the hill to Collins Street.
Walk west on Collins to Stafford. Turn right on Stafford and continue
to E. Mill, then turn left. Walk two blocks and turn right on Caroline
Street. Walk two blocks to Elizabeth Street and turn right. Turn right on
Smith Street, left on E. Main, and right on Stafford. Turn left on E. Mill
to return to the Plymouth Center.

Portage

One of Wisconsin's earliest settlements, connecting the Wisconsin and Fox rivers

Wisconsin's first highways were its rivers—the Mississippi, Wisconsin, Fox—and its earliest settlements were founded along these pathways. Portage grew up along the mile and a half portage trail between the Wisconsin and Fox rivers. This stretch of land enabled explorers and trappers to travel by water all the way from the East Coast to the Gulf of Mexico. In 1828, the U.S. Infantry built a fort at this location—Fort Winnebago—to protect the fur trade, and a decade later construction was begun on a canal to connect the rivers. The canal opened in 1851, opening the way for commercial barge traffic from Green Bay to Prairie du Chien. By the 1860s, Portage was selected as a regional railroad center, connecting it to Milwaukee, La Crosse, and Ashland. Portage was assured its place in the state's commercial development.

Portage's business district originated with several stores and residences located at the junction of

Detail, 101 W. Cook St.

Cook, Main, and DeWitt streets. The town was platted in 1852, incorporating as Portage City in 1854. At the center of the state's river and rail traffic, the city grew quickly—the two- and three-story brick business blocks you see today above Cook Street were in place by the late 1860s and 1870s. Mills, a tannery and foundry located on the south bank of the canal, is also in evidence today.

Portage remains a busy working town centered on Cook Street. A retail district tour requires you to dodge people and cars while looking upward for a glimpse of the city's past. Most buildings are brick, some red and some cream, and most are constructed in the Italianate style. The Michel building (1869-70) and the City Brewery (1851) occupy the corners of Cook and Wisconsin streets. The Michel Building, 136 W. Cook, housed a jewelry business until 1955. The building still exhibits cast iron window hoods and parapet. The brewery opposite was built by Carl Haertel, a native of Germany, who also

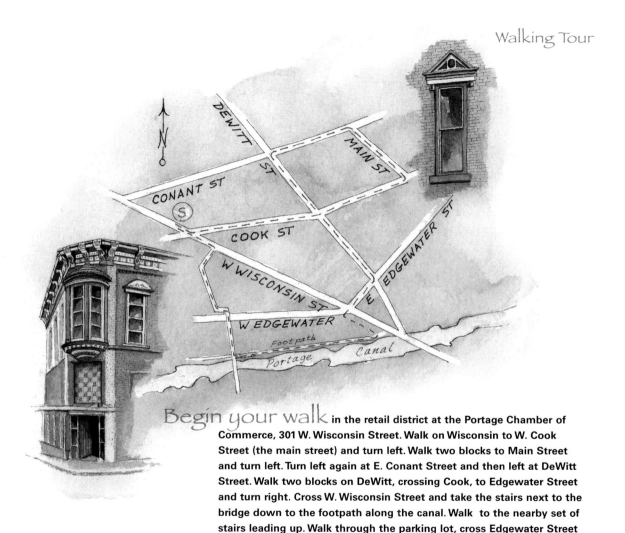

Begin your walk in the retail district at the Portage Chamber of Commerce, 301 W. Wisconsin Street. Walk on Wisconsin to W. Cook Street (the main street) and turn left. Walk two blocks to Main Street and turn left. Turn left again at E. Conant Street and then left at DeWitt Street. Walk two blocks on DeWitt, crossing Cook, to Edgewater Street and turn right. Cross W. Wisconsin Street and take the stairs next to the bridge down to the footpath along the canal. Walk to the nearby set of stairs leading up. Walk through the parking lot, cross Edgewater Street and cut across the block on the sidewalk. Coming out on Wisconsin, turn left and return to the chamber office.

built the handsome building at 135 W. Cook (1866) for his residence. By 1894, Haertel's home was converted to a retail location owned by clothiers employing as many as 50 tailors. Continuing down the block, notice the brick structure at 124 W. Cook (1869). Constructed by a brick manufacturer, the facade is enhanced by the original lines of the window lintels. The First National Bank moved

Footpath alongside the canal.

into a newly constructed building in 1893, at 101 W. Cook Street. The former bank fronts a round turret bay window over the corner, and some of the brick work reflects a Queen Anne influence.

The city's business district ran along DeWitt Street as well as Cook Street, between Conant Street and the canal. An excellent example of commercial Italianate is located at the corner of

DeWitt and Conant, 320 DeWitt Street (1889). The structure flaunts a wood cornice and brackets, projecting oriel windows, and cast iron columns at the angled entrance. Across the street at 305 DeWitt, the Beattie Building (1891) reflects much the same elaborate details. It was built by William Beattie, who produced and sold custom-made boots and shoes.

The city's landscape turns more industrial along the waterfront. At the end of DeWitt Street, the building at 201 DeWitt seems plain in comparison to its uptown neighbors. The storefront is original, as is its door and metal step. Take note of the large window on Edgewater Street facing the canal. Patrons of the lumber office paid for their goods through the 8-inch opening in this window.

A visit to Portage would not be complete without a short walk along the canal, accessible by the Wisconsin Street bridge. Stairs lead down to a gravel path that travels about a city block in length. Unmoving water and crumbling river bank do not do justice to the time the waterway was jammed with commercial barges and pleasure craft. Another set of stairs takes you up to a parking lot as you return to the center of activity in Portage today—its downtown streets.

Racine

A hard-working city with a gorgeous lakefront

A s you approach downtown Racine from the west, blue-collar neighborhoods surround you, reflecting the city's status as one of Wisconsin's most hard-working industrial hubs. But keep going till you reach Racine's heart —its easternmost point. Here, on the shores of Lake Michigan, curves a beautiful harbor, its watery sheen ruffled by wind and bobbing with boats. A landscaped park and festival grounds stand on the shore, and a historic lighthouse proudly sits at the end of a peninsula. Reclaimed and refurbished in the last 15 years, the lakefront is gorgeous, and a visual reminder that the city drew its life from the water.

Henry Miller House, 1110 Main St.

In 1828, Gilbert Knapp, then a captain in the Coast Guard, was convinced that of all the potential harbors on Lake Michigan, this site held the most promise. He established a claim in 1834 and two years later platted the town, north and south of where the Root River flowed into the lake. Settlers who followed him funded piers and dredging operations so that passenger ships and freighters could pull into port. By 1850, immigrants were pouring in, and Racine was exporting 1,500 bushels of wheat a day, second only to Chicago. Indeed, both Milwaukee and Chicago considered Racine a serious rival for commerce.

But then Racine broke stride. When railroads were needed to take goods to the frontier farther west, the other big port cities built theirs first. Racine's harbor grew quiet, and by World War I the last of its home ships had departed.

Manufacturing, though, grew strong. J.I. Case began making threshing machines in 1844. Other early settlers built wagons and buggies. By the turn of the century, citizens boasted that Racine manu-

mowers, metal casting and finishing, lithography and printing.

Thanks to ongoing restoration efforts, Racine's lakefront is a lovely place to stroll, especially on a

Joseph Miller House, 11th and Main St. **1228 Main St.**

factured more disparate articles than any other place of comparable size in the world. Many were known throughout the country: Johnson's Wax, Horlick's Malted Milk, Hamilton Beach appliances, Jacobsen lawn mowers, Oster blenders. Racine's economy was established. It still leads the nation in the manufacture of farm machinery and lawn

warm summer day when a cooling breeze fans off the lake. Main Street, the historic commercial district, contains a number of interesting buildings. The McClurg Building (1857) at 245 Main Street is perhaps the most striking, built with red brick and white stone. The offices of Racine's first railroad, it was also the site of the city's first library, first

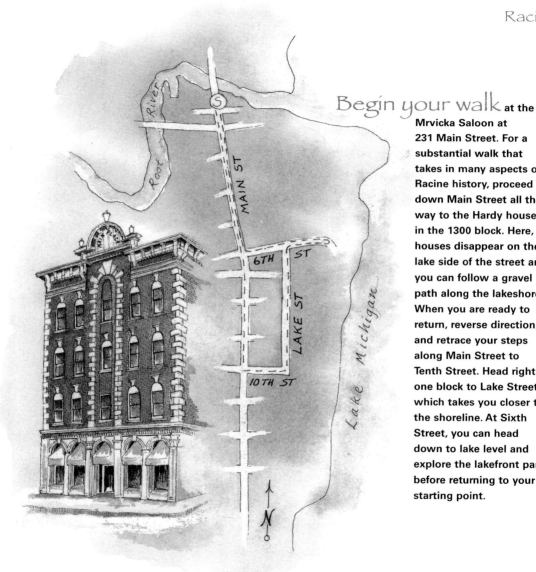

Begin your walk at the **Mrvicka Saloon at 231 Main Street. For a substantial walk that takes in many aspects of Racine history, proceed down Main Street all the way to the Hardy house in the 1300 block. Here, houses disappear on the lake side of the street and you can follow a gravel path along the lakeshore. When you are ready to return, reverse direction, and retrace your steps along Main Street to Tenth Street. Head right one block to Lake Street, which takes you closer to the shoreline. At Sixth Street, you can head down to lake level and explore the lakefront park before returning to your starting point.**

municipal court, first movie theater, and first Turkish bath, along with the country's first vocational school. A distinctive building of another sort is the Mrvicka Saloon (1891), built by the Pabst Brewery at 231 Main Street. Turrets askew, it has a charming but slightly tipsy appearance.

Hardy House, 1319 Main St.

At the intersection of Main and Sixth streets you find Monument Square. Called Market Square in 1837, it contained the town pump and was the place to buy and sell produce. Farther west are many of Racine's most elaborate homes. Among them are the Blake house (circa 1868) at 936 Main, former home of Lucius Blake, one of Racine's most important early industrialists; and the Olin house (1868) at 1144 S. Main, crowned with a lovely cupola that is used as the symbol for Preservation Racine. Notice, too, the Jones house (1850) at 1229 S. Main, a diminutive workman's cottage built before the neighborhood became affluent. And be sure to see the Hardy house (1905) at 1319 Main, designed by Wisconsin's most famous architect, Frank Lloyd Wright. For the best perspective, clamber down the adjacent bank to lake level and look up.

Racine has five buildings designed by Wright, and a number of others built in the Prairie style. To find these, pick up a tour guide at the Racine County Historical Society Museum at 701 Main Street. Another building worth detouring for is the Church of the Good Shepard (also called the Olympia Brown Unitarian Universalist Church) at 625 College Avenue, two blocks west of Main Street. Olympia Brown was the first American woman to be ordained with full denominational authority. Pastor of this congregation from 1878 to 1887, she resigned to become one of the state's most influential suffragists. Although Brown was not pastor when this church was built, she often spoke from its pulpit, as did Julia Ward Howe and Susan B. Anthony.

Rural

*A serene Yankee village
on the winding Crystal River*

One of Rural's favorite tales is of resident Tom Potts, who was so disturbed by the rush of new-fangled motor cars 75 or so years ago that he hauled his rocking chair into the road to slow everybody down. Rural, it seems, obeyed. Even today there is so little traffic in this tiny Waupaca County village you can walk unconcerned down the middle of the street.

That leaves you at leisure to admire the homes, a lovely, well-preserved collection of residences entwined, like string on a package, by the curving Crystal River. Unlike most Wisconsin communities, Rural never experienced an influx of European immigrants. The town was settled almost exclusively by Yankees of British heritage who moved here from the eastern United States. These founders stayed put, instead of moving farther west as was typical among the earliest settlers. Stable families, they preserved their pioneer homes, most of which were built in the Greek Revival style: square and spare, handsome and dignified, without the curlicues and gingerbread that adorn Victorian homes built later in the century. The result is a large—and rare—assembly of well-kept early architecture, and a village more evocative of New England than of the Midwest.

James Hinchman Jones arrived in the area in 1851, intent not on farming but on business, building a tavern and inn for travelers. He chose his site well, along a heavily traveled land route that connected the region's major waterways—the Wisconsin, the Fox, and the Wolf rivers. The sandy soil could support loaded freight wagons, and the Crystal River provided reliable water year

**Halfway House,
Rural's first home.**

round. Soon, Jones erected a mill, then named the place his "Rural Holdings."

For 20 years, Rural boomed. A lumber company moved in; so did a dry goods store and a

William Radley House.

millinery shop. Then the railroad passed the village by. Today, Rural is so far off the beaten track, many Wisconsin residents have never heard of it. Yet it's an exceptional place—one of only two towns in Wisconsin (Cooksville is the other) that has retained its Yankee pioneer character, with a personality so serene that visitors feel as if they've stepped back into the 19th century. An ever-flow-ing river winds through the village like a thread that will not be broken.

Rural's oldest house is Jones' Halfway House on the corner of Rural Road and Ashmun Street, built in 1852 where the wagon trail crossed the stream. Farther down Rural Road, tucked into a bend of the river, sits the second home to be built in the village, the Andrew Potts house (1853), now the Crystal River Inn. The Potts eventually expanded their holdings into a 370-acre farm; notice the huge barn next to the house. Across the street is the red-painted Jehudi Ashmun house (1858). Ashmun came to Rural as a young man, to visit his uncle and see what this interesting new country was like. He boarded at the Potts' house. So did Ellen Jones, the schoolmistress and daughter of founder James Hinchman Jones. "She is quite a case, and make no mistake," Jehudi wrote his family. When Jehudi and Ellen were married, her father built the house for them as a wedding present.

As you stroll around Rural, take note of the bridges that repeatedly cross the Crystal River. Built between 1900 and 1908, the stone and con-crete arched structures are themselves historic and some of the few remaining examples of their kind in the state.

Begin your walk on **Main Street at Rural's two adjacent stores,
Rural Artists (1898) and Weller's Store. Walk east on Main
Street past the town hall to Radley Street, then turn right to
head south on Radley. Turn right again on Rural Road, and
proceed west to the Crystal River Inn. To extend this very
short walk, head up the street just before the inn to the town
cemetery, where many of Rural's early settlers are buried.
Returning to Rural Road, turn left. Turn right on Main and
right again on Main to reach your starting point.**

Sheboygan Falls

An award-winner for historic preservation

It's hard to imagine the years when the storefronts of Sheboygan Falls were covered with "modern" plastic facades or boarded up and empty. Today, this little mill town along the banks of the Sheboygan River showcases perhaps the best collection of authentic historic restorations in the Midwest. In 1995 Sheboygan Falls became one of only five communities in the nation recognized as a Great American Main Street, an award presented annually by the National Trust for Historic Preservation.

"Falls," as it is locally dubbed, was originally settled by Yankees and New Yorkers in the days before Wisconsin was declared a state. Sheboygan Falls' founder, Colonel Silas Stedman, arrived in the area in 1835 and decided to stay because the "rapid waters of the Sheboygan River dashing down a very rocky ledge" offered an excellent source of water power, and the surrounding forest a source of lumber. Within a year Stedman had constructed a

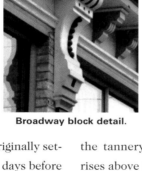

Broadway block detail.

sawmill, and in 1837 he purchased and platted the land along the riverbanks. By the mid-1800s Falls had eight sawmills, two woolen mills, and the first foundry between Milwaukee and Green Bay. Industries included hub and spoke factories and carriage and cabinet manufacturers. The community's prosperity was reflected in the Classic Greek Revival frame buildings gracing the business and residential districts.

Two sites remain today as evidence of the town's heritage, the Brickner Woolen Mill (1879) and the tannery, both located on the river. The mill rises above the rapids, dominating the commercial district. It operated on both water and steam power to produce woolen shawls, coats, suiting, dress goods, and blankets. Today, the converted mill is an apartment building. The tannery, upriver from the mill at 334 Broadway, was established in 1855, though the present brick structure was erected in 1880. Quality leather is still produced

Begin your walk on the east side of the river at the corner of Water and Adams streets. Walk one block north on Water to Monroe Street and turn left to walk across the bridge spanning the Sheboygan River. Turn left on Broadway and walk one and one-half blocks to a parking lot on your left, next to the Brickner Mill. On the river side of the parking lot you will find stairs that lead down to a small park with picnic table. Retrace your steps north along Broadway to Pine Street and turn left. Continue on Pine to the junction with Highway 32. Bear left, and shortly after that turn left on Elm Street. Walk along Elm Street to Buffalo and turn left. Continue down Buffalo to Maple and turn right. Reaching Broadway turn right, walk a short block to Monroe Street. Turn left and cross the bridge to return to your starting point.

here as it has been for over 100 years.

The downtown district between the mill and the tannery is a historic gem. The cream brick storefronts on Broadway and Pine streets have been meticulously restored to reflect their late-19th-century construction. The Joseph Osthelder Saloon (1878) at 513 Broadway features an original storefront complete with cast iron columns, and the

Odd Fellows Hall, 105 Pine St.

Odd Fellows Hall (1880) at 105 Pine shows fine detail work in the cornice crowning the second story.

Pine Street leads into the historic residential district, where the homes of Falls' prosperous merchants are located. Mill owner George Brickner built his home at 319 Elm in 1889. Brickner had served as a congressman in Washington, D.C., and patterned his neoclassic home after the White

House. The founder of the first woolen mill in town, William Prentice, built his home in 1870 at the corner of Detroit and Pine streets. The home was constructed in the Second Empire style popular on the East Coast at the time. The First Baptist Church, 735 Buffalo, was organized in 1838, making it the oldest Baptist church in Wisconsin. Constructed of white clapboard and sporting green shutters, it reflects the Yankee roots of Falls' first settlers, and it matches the style of three buildings found on the east side of the river.

Three pristine buildings stand in a row along Water Street, facing the Brickner Mill across the rapids. Mill House (1837), 516-518 Water Street, was the first frame home in the community. Built to house lumber company workers, it was also occupied for a time by Colonel Stedman. The Cole house (1842), 508 Water Street, was built by Charles Cole for his wife, Sarah, who taught school in the home. The Greek Revival building on the corner (1848), now a bed-and-breakfast, was built by Cole as a store. The first floor was used for retail, the second as living quarters, and the third as a meeting place for the founders of the first Temperance League in the Midwest. All three buildings have been authentically restored.

Stevens Point

A look at one of Wisconsin's most striking Polish communities

I t helps to bring a little imagination to Stevens Point's downtown. With a parking lot plopped in the middle of the public square, the scene has a decidedly modern appearance. But looking more carefully, you notice a wonderful set of 19th century buildings surrounding that rectangular plot. The morning sun shines brightly in the open space, casting both light and shadow on the aged brickwork, curving turrets and detailed cornices. You can see, too, an intriguing set of names etched in the storefronts: Bemowski, Czaplewski, Skow-

Christina Kuhl House, 1416 Main St.

ronski. The setting conjures up the hustle and bustle of an active marketplace and the lilting accents of hundreds of Polish voices.

Like so many northern Wisconsin towns, Stevens Point has its roots in the lumber industry. George Stevens arrived in this area by ox-drawn wagon and sent provisions from here up the Wisconsin River to his mill site near what is now Wausau. By 1839, he was using a log cabin at the river's edge as a kind of warehouse for goods being shipped northward. In 1845, Mathias Mitchell filed the town's original plat and established a tavern. This section of river soon proved a natural staging area. Provisions went upriver, rafts of timber came down, and Stevens Point grew, eventually earning the nickname "Gateway to the Pinery."

When the logging era ended, the power of the Wisconsin was harnessed for other uses. Papermaking, along with the manufacture of wooden sashes and doors, rose in prominence. Dams were built, the river was tamed, and the old slough was filled in. Farmers—primarily Polish immigrants—plowed the surrounding countryside. Some consider Stevens

Point, with its heritage of Polish newspapers, Polish churches, and Polish social halls, to have been the state's most characteristically Polish city. Even today, it has a Polish feel, and the Consolidated Paper Company still puffs smoke from its home along the banks of the Wisconsin River.

Grand Opera House, 1116-28 Main St.

The public square—once known for its mud and saloons—deserves a good look around. The Chilla Building (1892) at 1205-09 Second Street is the most prominent landmark. Once housing a community hall on its second floor, it features Palladian-inspired windows with rounded arches

and a central bay topped by a gleaming white dome. Also dominant is the Ossowski-Glinski Building (1890) at the intersection of Main and Second streets, with its large cupola and bell-shaped roof. The Polish-style mural of a rooster that adorns the wall of 836 Second Street is a charming accent note; it was painted in the 1970s by Bernice Bartosz, a retired schoolteacher and proofreader for the Polish newspaper, *Gwiazda Polarna*. The square, by the way, hosts the state's oldest farmer's market, which has run continuously here since 1870.

A stroll down Main Street leads to more interesting commercial buildings. The Bank of Stevens Point (1864) at 968 Main sports an elaborate metal cornice. The W.E. Ule Building (1904) at 1000 Main Street, with a brick cornice supported by a stone corbel, once housed two Polish newspapers. A lovely leaded-glass transom adorns the Kuhl Bros. Building (1873) at 1003 Main Street. A block down, the Grand Opera House (1894) at 1116-28 Main is impossible to overlook. Note the slotted brickwork, the heavy metal cornice, and inlaid metal panels with intersecting ovals. Also notice how tall the second-story windows are—evidence of the high-ceilinged interior.

Begin your walk in the public square at the
intersection of Main and Second streets. Examine the
buildings in the northern half of the square, then walk east
on Main Street to Strongs Avenue. Turn right and head
south one block on Strongs, then reverse direction and
return to Main. Turn left and walk west on Main Street
along the opposite side of the street so you get a good view
of the buildings on each side. When you reach the square,
examine the buildings on its southern perimeter before
returning to your starting point.

Stockholm

A tiny Swedish-American village on the shores of Lake Pepin

When Erik Petersson, a Swedish lumberjack, arrived on the shores of Lake Pepin in the mid-19th century, he decided to stay. The terraced bluffs and woodlands rising up from the lake—actually a broad bulge of the Mississippi River—reminded Petersson of his homeland, so he filed a land claim and sent word to his family he was founding a settlement here. A brother arrived in 1853 with a party of immigrants, and the follow-

Detail, Queen Anne, Third Street.

ing year Erik himself brought over a group of 200 Swedes. A 15-block village was platted in 1854, and its residents called it Stockholm. It was the first Swedish settlement in western Wisconsin.

The settlers thrived, selling grain, fish, cordwood and ice from the big lake. A small but substantial trade center developed with a handful of general stores and a hotel, blacksmith shop, grain

elevator, lumberyard, and several soft drink makers. The river, with its ferry lines, was the main highway to the outside world until the arrival of the railroad in 1886.

Stockholm's population reached 300 in 1900, but the 20th century brought change: riverboats snubbed the little town in favor of bigger cities. By 1940 the population dipped to 99, and it remains about the same today. However, the tiny town enjoyed a renaissance with the arrival of artists, crafters and antique dealers in the 1970s. Now Stockholm is a mecca for shoppers headed for galleries, shops and cafes. This new life swirls through a town preserved in the past.

Historic commercial buildings still line First Street (Highway 35) and Spring Street. One and two stories in height, most have tin roofs and false wooden fronts. The Merchants Hotel on Spring

Begin your walk at the junction of Highway 35 and Spring Street. Walk up Spring to Second Street and turn left. Turn left again on Vine Street. Halfway down the street, retrace your steps to Second Street and then to Spring Street, and head farther up the hill to Third Street. Turn right on Third Street, walk along it for three blocks, then retrace your path to Spring Street and your starting point.

Street (1867) hides stone walls behind its stucco surface. Long a hostelry, the hotel still caters to overnight visitors. A few doors down is the former Stockholm Post Office building, now housing historic memorabilia. The largest building in town,

from the 1860s are found along Vine Street, a block west from Spring Street. Running along the bluff above town, Second Street provides a spectacular setting for more historic homes. The walk from the business district is a bit of a climb, but

Former Post Office, Spring St.

Back of home, 194 Vine St.

located on the corner of Highway 35 and Spring Street, was Stockholm's general store. Now a retail store selling Amish goods, the second floor once housed an opera house complete with stage —harking back to the days when travelers disembarked from riverboats for an evening of dancing and performances.

Neat, mostly white clapboard homes line the residential streets. Greek Revival houses dating

well worth it. Here, on Church Hill crowned with the 1867 Evangelical Covenant Church, eight clapboard houses stand, framed by elms and old lilacs. Founder Erik Petersson's house (1872) is located at the southern end of the street.

The oldest home in Stockholm is the Great River Bed & Breakfast (1869) on Highway 35 at the east end of town. Built of stone, the home is now covered in stucco.

Sturgeon Bay
A Door County destination
shaped by its maritime history

Sturgeon Bay has been Door County's commercial hub since the 1850s. Sawmills and stone quarries, the early industries, gave way to shipbuilding after a canal was blasted along the Michigan-Sturgeon Bay portage in 1881. During the height of the 19th-century lumber boom, as many as 7,000 vessels a year traversed the canal between Lake Michigan and Green Bay. Today, shipbuilding cranes still fill the skyline above miles of waterfront, but the bay also is dotted with pleasure craft and lined with resorts and cottages. Sturgeon Bay

Fire Department, 38 S. Third Ave.

has become a tourist destination as well as a blue-collar port.

Sturgeon Bay began as a fur trading outpost when Increase Claflin established a post at Little

Sturgeon in 1835, becoming the area's first resident. The first influx of settlers, Yankees and Norwegian immigrants, arrived in the 1850s to work in the sawmills located along the waterfront (today's commercial district). Stone quarrying and ice harvesting helped diversify the economy. The construction of the Sturgeon Bay-Lake Michigan canal brought prosperity to the little town, allowing ships filled with lumber and wood products to avoid the dangerous Port des Morts Strait 100 miles to the north.

The shipbuilding industry dates back to the 1880s when the firm of Leathem and Smith began boat construction and repairs. Shipbuilding expanded greatly during World War II, when ships were built for the Navy. Today the Palmer-Johnson Company enjoys an international reputation for building luxury oceangoing yachts for clients such as the King of Spain and the late Shah of Iran.

Church on the corner of Louisiana Street and Fifth Avenue is of particular interest, built in the Romanesque Revival style. Many of the houses in

Greisen Building, 160 N. 3rd Ave.

Schimmel Building, 139 N. 3rd Ave.

Sturgeon Bay contains two historic districts, both listed in 1983 on the National Register of Historic Places. The first is the Louisiana/Seventh Avenue Historic District, a charming, tree-shaded residential neighborhood that boasts two dozen 19th- and early-20th-century houses and one church complex. St. Joseph's Roman Catholic

the historic district were built in the late Queen Anne style. The Richard P. Cody house (1903) at 16 N. Fifth Avenue is a good example, as is the residence at 551 Louisiana Street. Note the intricate wood detail in the dormer and the rounded corner porch. The Charles Reynolds house (1850) at 552 Louisiana Street is one of the oldest houses in the

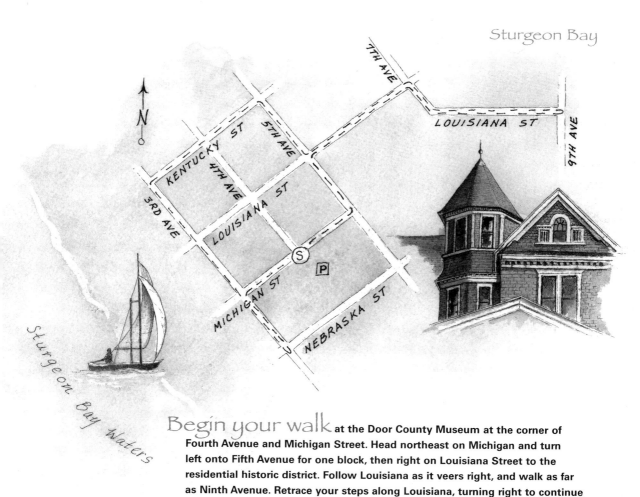

Begin your walk at the Door County Museum at the corner of Fourth Avenue and Michigan Street. Head northeast on Michigan and turn left onto Fifth Avenue for one block, then right on Louisiana Street to the residential historic district. Follow Louisiana as it veers right, and walk as far as Ninth Avenue. Retrace your steps along Louisiana, turning right to continue along Fifth Avenue to Kentucky Street. Turn left on Kentucky and walk all the way to Third Avenue and the commercial district. Turn left and follow Third Avenue three blocks to Nebraska Street. Then backtrack along Third Avenue to Michigan Street, and turn right to return to your starting point.

Friends Church, 204 W. Maple St.

which runs from Kentucky to Nebraska streets. It has been nicely restored with frequently spaced benches for tired walkers and period street lamps. The attractive use of paint draws attention to the architectural details of these historic buildings, and if you look up above the modern storefronts you see some of the names of the original builders. The Sturgeon Bay commercial district lost 12 buildings to fire in 1880, including the village hall and firehouse. These were rebuilt in brick and stone in the Italianate, Queen Anne, and Classical Revival styles that were popular from 1880 until 1910. Builders made frequent use of the locally quarried gray limestone.

The A. N. Wagener commercial block (circa 1885-91) at 13-23 N. Third Avenue was built in the Queen Anne style and features carved wooden columns and lovely decorative detail above the storefronts and around the windows. The F. Conjurske Building (1905-06) at 36 N. Third Avenue uses local limestone in its Classical Revival style construction. The stone detail at the top of the building surely sets it apart from its neighbors. The John Masse Hardware Building (1872) at 22 S. Third Avenue is one of the few frame structures in the historic district that escaped the fire of 1880.

district, with gleaming white clapboard siding and attractive arched windows. The Hope Congregational Parsonage (1890) at 48 N. Eighth Avenue, with its interesting porch, is a good example of an American Foursquare.

The second area listed on the National Register is the Third Avenue Downtown Historic District,

Watertown

A proud, old city perched on the banks of the Rock River

E verywhere you look in Watertown there are beautiful old buildings of cream-colored brick. You can understand the pride its citizens feel in their rich heritage. It shows in the care they take in their historic neighborhoods. The existence of so many preserved brick buildings gives the city a unified appearance and allows you to imagine the way the city looked 100 years ago.

Watertown was settled in 1836, with a dam constructed on the Rock River the following year. Sawmills, flour mills, and a woolen mill soon followed. Watertown became

St. Bernards Catholic Church, 114 S. Church St.

a city in 1853, and soon grew to be the second largest community in the state, due mainly to the construction of Watertown Plank Road from Milwaukee. A wave a German immigrants followed,

and by the Civil War, Watertown was predominantly German. After 1847, brick making flourished, and the distinctive, cream-colored "Watertown" brick was used for many of the city's buildings.

South of the historic Main Street commercial area, and east of the river, lies what was a fashionable residential area in the 1850s surrounding a public square. The square was part of the original platting of the city. A Civil War monument was erected on the site in 1899 and the square was renamed Memorial Park. Surrounding this lovely little park are residences dating to the latter half of the 19th century and built in a variety of styles popular at the time: Queen Anne, Italianate, and Colonial Revival, with some homes exhibiting an eclectic mix of styles reflecting the tastes of their owners.

A beautifully restored Queen Anne, with brick porch and high gables ornamented with decorative shingles, can be seen at 701 S. Fourth Street, where you begin your walk. The streets are narrow

Residence built of Watertown brick.

and tree-shaded, and it is easy to imagine the area without modern cars and buildings. At 512 S. Fifth Street, Herman Grube, one-time mayor of Watertown, built his house between 1897 and 1900. The cream brick Queen Anne features elab-

orate leaded glass windows and an unusual band of corbelled brick work at the top of the elevations. The Pugh home at 501 S. Fourth Street was built prior to 1886. It is primarily Italianate in style with Second Empire variations, such as the concave roof over the entry topped with ornate iron work. At 410 S. Fourth Street you find the Brandt-Quirk home (1875), a modified Greek Revival. It has been well maintained and is now operated as a bed-and-breakfast.

Most of the homes along S. Third Street were built in the 1880s and 1890s. The house at 500 S. Third Street has been restored, its gardens well tended and complete with horse hitch and carriage step. It is listed on the National Register of Historic Places. The Fred Miller house (circa 1889) at 600 S. Third Street, built for the president of the Wisconsin National Bank, is a noteworthy Queen Anne, with beautiful stained glass windows and an open spindle porch.

The area's churches, while not on the walk, are worth noting. One, St. Paul's Episcopal (1859) at 413 S. Second Street, was built in the Gothic Revival style and added to in 1885 and 1931. It is possible to admire its steep gable roof and spire from a vantage spot in Memorial Park.

Begin your walk **at the southeast corner of Memorial Park at the intersection of S. Fourth and Milwaukee streets. Stroll south along S. Fourth Street for a block and turn left on Western Avenue. Turn left again onto S. Fifth Street and walk past the Herman Grube house at number 512. Turn left on Spring Street then right on S. Fourth Street at the Brandt-Quirk home at number 410. Walk for one block, then turn left on Dodge Street. Turn left onto S. Third Street and enjoy the fine houses that dot the next three blocks. Turn left on Milwaukee Street, which takes you back to your starting point.**

Wausau
One of northern Wisconsin's largest cities,
built by the lumber industry

Today, as always, the Wisconsin River dominates Wausau, snaking through the city like a powerful cobra. Though controlled by dams and crossed by bridges, its muscle is abundantly clear: Right through the heart of Wausau runs a world championship whitewater kayaking course, sustained by the frothy, rushing waters that once powered mills for sawing timber.

Wausau is a product of the pinery. In 1836, a treaty transferred a strip of land along the Wisconsin River from the Menominee Tribe to the U.S. government. Two years later, lumber barons in St. Louis sent George Stevens to investigate the area's potential. "It is decidedly the best Mill Site I ever saw or heard of in the Union," Stevens wrote back. The community that developed called itself Big Bull Falls, after its roaring rapids, and by 1850, 14 sawmills were processing the huge rafts of logs that were floated downriver from North Woods lumber camps.

**Ely Wright House,
901 Sixth St.**

As more settlers arrived, the more respectable name "Wausau"—which means "far away place" in Chippewa—was adopted. The arrival of the railroad spurred even more wood-related industries. Farmers worked the surrounding countryside (most notably, for dairying and the growing of ginseng), with Wausau serving as the hub of commerce. Gradually, it became one of the north's largest cities and remains so today.

Unfortunately, almost all of the structures associated with Wausau's lumbering days have been torn down. Gone too are many of the old commercial buildings that once lined the downtown streets. A pedestrian mall has preserved some of them, however, and nearby lies a lovely historic district filled with beautiful homes built for Wausau's wealthiest citizens in the late 18th and early 19th centuries.

Of these, the most well known is the Cyrus C. Yawkey house (1901) at 403 McIndoe Street, built

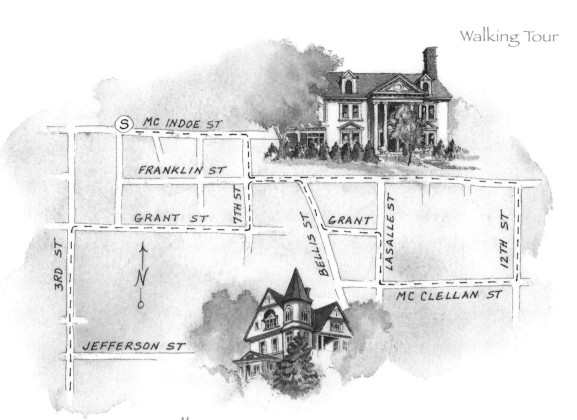

Begin your walk at the Leigh Yawkey house at 403 McIndoe Street. Head east on McIndoe to Seventh Street, then turn right and walk south one block to Franklin. Turn left to continue east—up East Hill—on Franklin to 12th Street, where you turn right to find the Leigh Yawkey Woodson Art Museum. Walk south on 12th Street to McClellan, then turn right to walk down East Hill and through Stewart Park. A right on LaSalle and a left on Grant takes you to a view of the railroad depot. From here you can either take the pathless route and go directly across the railroad tracks and around the depot to continue west on Grant, or turn right on Bellis Street, left on Franklin Street going west, and left on Seventh Street to reconnect with Grant to your right. However you get there, follow Grant west to Third Street, where you turn left and walk south to explore the commercial area. To return to your starting point, walk north on Third to McIndoe and turn right.

for the lumber magnate and industrialist. Now the headquarters of the Marathon County Historical Society, it features Ionic columns, a pedimented portico, and a pleasing formal garden. A look inside the house is highly recommended, if only to see the gorgeous honey-colored woodwork crafted of curly birch hand-selected from the Yawkey mill.

Cyrus Yawkey House, 403 McIndoe St.

Up the side of East Hill stretches a neighborhood of wide streets and spacious homes. Among the most magnificent: the very pink Queen Anne (1887) built for lumberman Samuel Knox at 504 Franklin Street; the Italianate Ely Wright house (1881) at 901 Sixth Street, built for the founder of the Wausau Iron Works (note the decorative window caps); and the two Victorian mansions, one blue, one green, that sit across from each other at

the intersection of LaSalle and McClellan streets. It's at this intersection that you also find the entrance to Stewart Park. This gracious green space, with a stone amphitheater, gates, and walls, is set into the steeply sloping hill, with white pine trees forming a natural canopy. In the 1920s, young female dancers performed here, influenced, no doubt, by Isadora Duncan. Other landmarks of the neighborhood are the Milwaukee Road Depot (1902) at 720 Grant Street, known throughout the nation as the symbol of the Wausau Insurance Company; and a log cabin (1902) at 802 McClellan Street that housed the printing machinery of the Philosopher Press. Local intellectuals gathered here to discuss literature, art, and politics.

Downtown, the 300 block of Main Street has been converted to a pleasant pedestrian mall, highlighted by the Livingston/Winkelman Building (1904) at 300 Main Street. It has an outstanding brick facade and a banding of chevrons ("W" stands for "Winkelman," not "Wausau"). Note, too, the Kryshak Cigar Factory building at 310 Third Street. Kryshak's catered to the wealthy, and was considered the state's most prestigious cigar house. The factory operated on the upper floors; a saloon called "The Odd" occupied the building's street level.

Whitewater

A college town, architecturally serene,
yet bustling with students

In Whitewater, education dominates: the University of Wisconsin—Whitewater is the town's largest employer. Learning is unusually accessible, too. In this small village, students can walk between home and classroom from their first day of kindergarten till graduate school commencement. Perhaps that's why Whitewater feels so stately and serene. The streets are broad, the houses capacious—like minds open to new ideas. The only activity is that of students scurrying to get to class on time.

Engebretsen-Dorr House, 622 W. Main St.

The town takes its name from a Potawatomi word, *waubegannawpocat*, which means "white water" and refers to the whitish sand that lies on the bottom of nearby creeks. When Zerah Mead arrived in 1837, he found the area delightful. "The old burr oak trees looked like orchards, the wild flowers were in gorgeous bloom, and the whole country looked like some gentleman's fancy park."

(It was less charming, no doubt, to Abraham Lincoln, who five years earlier had his horse stolen here and had to complete a trip to Peoria on foot.)

By 1838 enough wheat was being harvested that a gristmill was deemed urgent. Only one suitable site existed, so the citizens demanded that its owner either give bonds to build the mill or relinquish his claim. He relinquished, and a new owner, committed to the mill, was sought and found. It is said that settlers from four towns raised the mill's frame, followed by an outdoor feast and ball games on the prairie. Even today, evidence of the mill's importance to these early pioneers remains. You can't help but notice Whitewater's odd street pattern: Primary thoroughfares radiate like sunbeams from the old mill site.

Town growth accelerated after the railroad arrived in 1852. With eight trains arriving daily, the railroad depot was a hub of activity. Built in

1890, the vermillion-colored Victorian building is beautifully restored and now houses the Whitewater Historical Society Museum.

Hamilton House, Second Empire, 328 W. Main St.

Winchester Wagon Works, Esterly Reaper Works, and the Trippe and Combie Paper Mill were all important industries. Between 1852 and 1853, 77 buildings went up; by 1860 there were 412. In 1868, the Whitewater Normal School, predecessor of UW-Whitewater, opened with nine faculty members and 48 pupils. The Morris Pratt Institute, a more unusual facility, was founded in 1902. Pratt, according to a local historian, be-

lieved he had accumulated his fortune through the guidance of "invisible intelligences." Out of gratitude, he established an institute in which to hold seances and proffer "services in the interests of Spiritualism."

Today, you'll find some of Whitewater's finest buildings in the neighborhood that lies between the university and downtown, with many of them now home to fraternities and sororities. The Engebretsen-Dorr house (1895) at 622 Main Street is lavishly covered with brackets, gables, fanbursts and shingles of all shapes. Look for the former home of G.W. Esterly, son of the founder of the Esterly Reaper Works, at 604 W. Main Street (1876). Notice too the matching carriage house behind it. Remodeled in 1919 as a home, it is one of the few extant brick carriage houses in the state. At 328 Main Street, the Hamilton house (1868) is a vision. Built in the Second Empire style and decorated with Queen Anne spool and spindle work, it is considered one of the finest examples of its type in the state. Other features to note in town are Birge Fountain (1903), with its nymphs, cherubs and dolphins; and at the corner of Main and Franklin, the Territorial burr oak, measured by government surveyors in 1836.

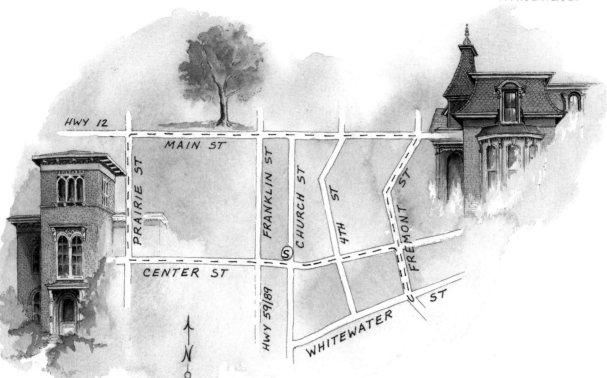

Begin your walk at the delightful Smith-Allen house (1856) at
445 Center Street, where Center intersects with Church Street. Walk
west along Center to Prairie Street, then turn right, heading north
on Prairie to Main Street. Turn right again and stroll down Main
Street to Fremont Street. Turn right on Fremont and walk three
blocks to its intersection with Whitewater Street, where you find
the railroad depot. To return to your starting point, reverse direction
and head back on Fremont Street as far as Center Street. Turn left and
proceed west on Center to Church Street.

For More Information

Many of the places listed in this book have walking tours sponsored by local organizations. For more information on historic walks, contact:

Buffalo County Historical Society
Box 87, Alma, WI 54610   (608) 685-6290

**Old Third Ward
Neighborhood Association, Inc.**
523 South State St., Appleton, WI 54911
(920) 733-5766

Sauk County Historical Society
531 4th Ave., Baraboo, WI 53913   (608) 356-1001

Bayfield Chamber of Commerce
P.O. Box 138, Bayfield, WI 54814-0138
(715) 779-3335 / (800) 447-4094

**Chamber of Commerce
Business Improvement District**
P.O. Box 128, Berlin, WI 54923   (920) 361-3636

Cassville Chamber of Commerce
P.O. Box 576, Cassville, WI 53806   (608) 725-5855

Cassville Historical Society
P.O. Box 125, Cassville, WI 53806   (608) 725-5210

Cedarburg Chamber of Commerce
W63 N645 Washington Ave., Cedarburg, WI   53012
(414) 377-9620 / (800) 237-2874

Chippewa Falls Main Street Association
P.O. Box 554, Chippewa Falls, WI 54729
(715) 723-6661/7858

Cooksville Historic Tours
sponsored/supported by Union Bank & Trust Co.
P.O. Box 15, Evansville, WI 53536   (608) 882-5200

**Eau Claire Area Convention
& Visitors Bureau**
3625 Gateway Dr., #F, Eau Claire, WI 54701-8187
(715) 831-2345 / (800) 344-FUN

Ephraim Information Center
P.O. Box 203, Ephraim, WI 54211   (920) 854-4989

Evansville Chamber of Commerce
P.O. Box 51, Evansville, WI 53536-0051 (608) 882-5131

Brown County Historical Society
P.O. Box 1411, Green Bay, WI 54305-1411
(920) 437-1840

**Hudson Area Chamber of Commerce
& Tourism Bureau**
502 Second St., Hudson, WI 54016
(715) 386-8411 / (800) 657-6775

Janesville Historic Commission
18 North Jackson St., Janesville, WI 53547
(608) 755-3085/3065

**Kenosha Area Convention
& Visitors Bureau**
812 56th St., Kenosha, WI 53140
(414) 658-4FUN / (800) 654-7309

Kenosha Historical Museum
6300 Third Ave., Kenosha, WI 53143   (414) 654-5770

**La Crosse Area Convention
& Visitors Bureau**
410 East Veterans Memorial Dr., La Crosse, WI 54601
(608) 782-2366

Lake Geneva Chamber of Commerce
201 Wrigley Dr., Lake Geneva, WI 53147
(414) 248-4416 / (800) 345-1020

**Greater Madison Convention
& Visitors Bureau**
615 E. Washington Ave. Madison, WI 53703
(608) 255-2537 / (800) 373-6376

Historic Milwaukee, Inc.
P.O. Box 511220, Milwaukee, WI 53203-0211
(414) 277-7795

Mineral Point Historical Society
P.O. Box 188, Mineral Point, WI 53565   (608) 987-2884

Platteville Chamber of Commerce
P.O. Box 16, Platteville, WI 53818-0016 (608) 348-8888

Plymouth Chamber of Commerce
P.O. Box 584, Plymouth, WI 53073   (920) 893-0079

Portage Chamber of Commerce
301 W. Wisconsin St., Portage, WI 53901
(608) 742-6242

Racine County Historical Museum
701 Main St. - South, Racine, WI 53403
(414) 636-3926

Rural Historical Society
c/o Ann Harvey, 1437 Rural Rd., Waupaca, WI 54981

Sheboygan Falls Chamber Main Street, Inc.
641 Monroe St., Suite 108,
Sheboygan Falls, WI 53085   (920) 467-6206

**Stevens Point Area Convention
& Visitors Bureau**
23 Park Ridge Dr., Stevens Point, WI 54481
(715) 344-2556

Stockholm Tourism
P.O. Box 36, Stockholm, WI 54769   (715) 442-2015

**Sturgeon Bay Community
Development Corporation**
P.O. Box 212, Sturgeon Bay, WI 54235
(920) 743-6246

Watertown Area Chamber of Commerce
519 East Main St., Watertown, WI 53094
(920) 261-6320

Marathon County Historical Society
410 McIndoe St., Wausau, WI 54403
(715) 848-6143

Whitewater Area Chamber of Commerce
P.O. Box 34, Whitewater, WI 53190-0034
(414) 473-4005

Trailblazer ($250,000 or more)
AT&T
Credit Unions of Wisconsin
SC Johnson Wax

Voyageur ($75,000 or more)
Firstar Corporation
Harley-Davidson, Inc.
Marshall & Ilsley Corporation
Outdoor Advertising Association
Philip Morris Companies: Miller Brewing Company,
Kraft Foods/Oscar Mayer Foods Corp., Philip Morris USA
W. H. Brady Co.
Wisconsin Manufacturers & Commerce

Founder ($30,000 or more)
ANR Pipeline Company
Blue Cross/Blue Shield United Wisconsin
Color Ink, Inc.
DEC International, Inc.
General Casualty
Home Savings
John Deere Horicon Works
Johnson Controls
Kikkoman Foods, Inc.
Kohler Co.
Marcus Theatres Corporation
Michael, Best & Friedrich
Midwest Express Airlines
Nicolet Minerals Company
Northwestern Mutual Life Foundation
Promega Corporation
Robert W. Baird & Co., Inc.
Snap-on Incorporated
Time Insurance
Weber-Stephen Company
Weyerhaeuser
Wisconsin Central Ltd.
Wisconsin Power & Light Foundation
Wisconsin Public Service Foundation
Wisconsin State Cranberry Growers Association

Badger ($10,000 or more)
3M
Aid Association for Lutherans
Allen-Edmonds Shoe Corporation
A.O. Smith Corporation
Badger Mining Corporation
Briggs & Stratton Corporation
Case Corporation
Consolidated Papers, Inc.
Dairyland Power Cooperative
Edgewater Hotel
Eller Media Company
Fort James Corporation
Fraser Papers
Green Bay Packaging, Inc.
International Paper
Jockey International, Inc.
Jorgensen Conveyors, Inc.
Kimberly-Clark Corporation
Mann Bros., Inc.
Marathon Communications
Marcus Corporation
Marshfield Clinic
Modine Manufacturing Company
National Business Furniture, Inc.
Oscar J. Boldt Construction Co.
Pizza Pit, Ltd.
Rockwell Automation/Allen-Bradley
Rust Environment & Infrastructure
ShopKo
Stevens Point Brewery
Twin Disc, Incorporated
United States Cellular
Wausau and Mosinee Papers
Wisconsin Counties Association
Virchow, Krause & Company, LLP

More Books From Wisconsin Trails

Paddling Northern Wisconsin
Mike Svob

W Is for Wisconsin (child's book)
Dori Hillestad Butler / Illustrated by Eileen Dawson

Portrait of the Past
A Photographic Journey Through Wisconsin 1865-1920
Howard Mead, Jill Dean and Susan Smith

The W-Files
True Reports of Wisconsin's Unexplained Phenomena
Jay Rath

Great Wisconsin Restaurants
Dennis Getto

The Wisconsin Traveler's Companion
A Guide to Country Sights
Jerry Apps / Illustrated by Julie Sutter-Blair

Great Wisconsin Walks
Wm. Chad McGrath

Great Weekend Adventures
The Editors of Wisconsin Trails

County Parks of Wisconsin
Jeannette & Chet Bell

Best Canoe Trails of Southern Wisconsin
Michael E. Duncanson

Best Wisconsin Bike Trips
Phil Van Valkenberg

Barns of Wisconsin
Jerry Apps

Wisconsin The Story of the Badger State
Norman K. Risjord